NDPS ACT - SUPREME COURT'S LATEST LEADING CASE LAWS

CASE NOTES- FACTS- FINDINGS OF APEX COURT JUDGES & CITATIONS

JAYPRAKASH BANSILAL SOMANI

Dedicated

To

All the Past & Present Judges of the Supreme Court of India.

Salute to their wisdom.

Salute to their interpretation of Law.

Salute to their elaborative judgement writing.

Contents

Contents

Preface

Dear Learned Advocates of the Trial Courts, Session Courts, High Courts, Supreme Court & Individuals,

I am very delighted to provide you a book on 'NARCOTIC DRUGS AND PSYCHOTROPIC SUBSTANCES (NDPS) ACT' - Supreme Court of India's Latest Leading Case Laws'.

In this book you will get...

1. Name of the Case i. e. Cause title

2.Relevant Sections discussed in the case

3. Hon'ble Judges/Coram of the case

4.Number of PDF Pages in Original Judgement of the case

5. All available Citations of the case

6. Case Note with appeal allowed/ dismissed or disposed off

7. Facts of the case

8. Hon'ble Apex Court's findings, while dismissing/allowing or disposing the appeal

9. Ratio Decidendi if any.

My special thanks to Manupatra, because of their web portal I can compile this book in well manner. I am also thankful to Notion Press to support me to publish & market this book throughout the Country. Thanks to my Juniors, Advocate Colleagues & Insolvency Professional Colleagues to support me in this venture.

Miss Devpriya Shah has helped me a lot to compile this book.

I hope this book will add some value addition in the wealth of your legal knowledge. Your positive feedbacks will boost me to compile/ write further books & negative feedbacks will improve my skills. Kindly send your valuable feedbacks by email.

Thanks with Regards,

Jayprakash B. Somani
Advocate, Supreme Court of India
Email: jaysomani64@gmail.com
Web Site:www.jayprakashsomani.com
Call: 8384051134, 9322188701, 8459194576

Acknowledgements

Printed & Published by
Notion Press
No. 8, 3rd Cross Street,
CIT Colony, Mylapore,
Chennai, Tamil Nadu- 600004

Managed by
Jayprakash Somani Advocates & Solicitors
Law Firm for Supreme Court of India
Delhi Office
257 C, Pocket 1, Mayur Vihar Phase 1, Delhi 110091.
Call 8384051134, 9322188701, 8459194576
Supreme Court Chamber
312, 3rd Floor, M. C. Setalvad Block, In front of 'D' Gate, Bhagwan Das Road, Supreme Court of India, New Delhi 110001
Contact: 8459194576, 9811011747
www.jayprakashsomani.com

Books are available online in India
1. **Notion Press:**https://notionpress.com/author/jayprakash_somani
2. **Amazon:**https://www.amazon.in/s?k=jayprakash+somani
3. **Flipkart:**https://www.flipkart.com/search?q=Jayprakash%20Somani

Books are available online at International Market
4. **Amazon International:** https://www.amazon.com/s?k=jayprakash+somani
5. **Amazon United Kingdom:** https://www.amazon.co.uk/s?k=jayprakash+somani
6. **E-Books/Kindle edition at National & International Level:** https://www.amazon.in/s?k=jayprakash+somani

CHAPTER ONE

Bharat Chaudhary and Ors. Vs. Union of India (UOI) and Ors., 2021

Hon'ble Judges/Coram:

N.V. Ramana, C.J.I., Surya Kant and Hima Kohli, JJ.

Equivalent Citation: 2022(379)ELT34(S.C.), 2022(1)RCR(Criminal)490, MANU/SC/1240/2021

Relevant Section/provisions: Section 439 of the Code of Criminal Procedure, 1973; Sections 8(c), 22(c), 25, 28, 29, 67 of the Narcotic Drugs and Psychotropic Substances Act, 1985

Number of Pages in the Original Judgment:: 05

Case Note:

Criminal - Bail - Section 439 of the Code of Criminal Procedure, 1973 (CrPC) - Sections 8(c), 22(c), 25, 28, 29, 67 of the Narcotic Drugs and Psychotropic Substances Act, 1985 (NDPS Act) - A4 arrested pursuant to confessional statement made by A1 - Special Judge granted bail to A4 - High Court vide impugned judgment reversed the findings and cancelled bail granted - Appellant contended that High Court committed grave error by completely overlooking the fact that not a single tablet was recovered from the possession of A4 - Tablets were seized from the premises of A-1 to A-3 - Whether High Court erred in reversing the order granting bail to A4 who contended to have been dragged based on confessional statement?

Brief Facts:

The prosecution contended that on specific information received by the Directorate of Revenue Intelligence (DRI) seized about 1,37,665 tablets of different types described as psychotropic substances from different locations. Arrests of accused named made. A4 was granted bail. However, in appeal, High Court cancelled the bail. Hence, the present appeal.

Held, while disposing the Petition:

Impugned order cancelling the bail granted in favour of A-4 is not sustainable in view of the fact that the records sought to be relied upon by the prosecution show that one test report dated 6th December, 2019, two test reports dated 17th December, 2019 and one test report dated 21st December, 2019 in respect of the sample pills/tablets drawn and sent for testing by the prosecuting agency conclude with a note appended by the Assistant Commercial Examiner at the foot of the reports stating that "quantitative analysis of the samples could not be carried out for want of facilities". In the absence of any clarity so far on the quantitative analysis of the samples, the prosecution cannot be heard to state at this preliminary stage that the Petitioners have been found to be in possession of commercial quantity of psychotropic substances as contemplated under the NDPS Act.

In the absence of any psychotropic substance found in the conscious possession of A-4, mere reliance on the statement made by A-1 to A-3 under Section 67 of the NDPS Act is too tenuous a ground to sustain the impugned order.

Petitions for special leave to appeal are disposed of accordingly.

CHAPTER TWO

Union of India (UOI) through Narcotics Control Bureau, Lucknow Vs. Md. Nawaz Khan, 2021

Hon'ble Judges/Coram:

Dr. D.Y. Chandrachud and B.V. Nagarathna, JJ.

Equivalent Citation: 2021(227)AIC1, AIR2021SC4476, 2021 (3) ALT (Crl.) 270 (A.P.), 2022(1)BLJ211, 2021(4)Crimes1(SC), 2021(378)ELT245(S.C.), 2021(4)J.L.J.R.66, 2021(5)JKJ309[SC], 2021(4)PLJR26, (2021)10SCC100, MANU/SC/0689/2021

Relevant Section/provisions: Sections 8, 21, 27A, 29 of the Narcotic Drugs and Psychotropic Substances Act, 1985

Number of Pages in the Original Judgment: 10

Case Note:

Narcotics - Cancellation of Bail - Offence allegedly committed under Sections 8, 21, 27A, 29 of the Narcotic Drugs and Psychotropic Substances Act, 1985 (Act) - High Court vide impugned order allowed Respondent's application for bail - Whether Respondent wrongly granted bail considering nature and gravity of offence?

Brief Facts:

Respondent before the High Court contended that he was only a companion in the vehicle which was driven by co-Accused and was not in conscious possession of the contraband since it had been recovered from the wiper fitted on the front bonnet of the vehicle, of which he had no knowledge. Moreover, it was urged that the provisions of Sections 42 and 50 of the NDPS Act were not complied with. According to the Respondent, the statement under Section 67 had not been duly explained to him, which was evident from the fact that the official of the SSB who signed it had certified that the translation had been explained in Manipuri to co-Accused.

Held, while allowing the Appeal:

i. The test which the High Court and this Court are required to apply while granting bail is whether there are reasonable grounds to believe that the Accused has not committed an offence and whether he is likely to commit any offence while on bail. Given the seriousness of offences punishable under the NDPS Act and in order to curb the menace of drug-trafficking in the country, stringent parameters for the grant of bail under the NDPS Act have been prescribed.
ii. The following circumstances are crucial to assessing whether the High Court has correctly evaluated the application for bail, having regard to the provisions of Section 37: (i) The Respondent was travelling in the vehicle all the way from Dimapur in Nagaland to Rampur in Uttar Pradesh with the co-Accused; (ii) The complaint notes that the CDR analysis of the mobile number used by the Respondent indicates that the Respondent was in regular touch with the other Accused persons who were known to him; (iii) The quantity of contraband found in the vehicle is of a commercial quantity; and (iv) The contraband was concealed in the vehicle in which the Respondent was travelling with the co-Accused.
iii. The impugned order of the High Court, apart from observing that no contraband was found from the personal search of the Respondent has ignored the above circumstances.
iv. The High Court has clearly overlooked crucial requirements and glossed over the circumstances which were material to the issue as to whether a case for the grant of bail was established. The High Court ought to have given due weight to the seriousness and gravity of the crime which it has failed to do.
v. Appeal allowed and the impugned judgment and order of the High Court set aside.

CHAPTER THREE

Jeet Ram Vs.The Narcotics Control Bureau, Chandigarh, 2020

Hon'ble Judges/Coram:

Ashok Bhushan, R. Subhash Reddy and M.R. Shah, JJ.

Equivalent Citation: 2021(1)ACR459, 2020(215)AIC34, AIR2020SC4313, 2020 (2) ALD(Crl.) 1009 (SC), 2021 (114) ACC 692, 2020(6)BLJ89, 2020CriLJ4694, 2021(1)Crimes177(SC), 2020(5)JKJ238[SC], 2020(4)RCR(Criminal)151, 2020(4)RLW3014(SC), 2021 (1) SCJ 557, 2020(3)UC1388, MANU/SC/0684/2020

Relevant Section/provisions: Section of 20 of Narcotic Drugs and Psychotropic Substances Act, 1985

Number of Pages in the Original Judgment: 08

Case Note:

Criminal - Conviction - Challenge against thereto - Section of 20 of Narcotic Drugs and Psychotropic Substances Act, 1985 ('NDPS Act')- Trial Court acquitted the Appellant on the ground of infirmities in prosecution version - High Court in appeal reversed the verdict and instead convicted the Appellant by impugned judgment - Hence, the present Appeal - Whether High Court while reappreciating the evidence rightly reversed the reasoned order of Trial Court?

Brief Facts:

The Appellant-Accused was tried for a charge punishable under Section 20 of Narcotic Drugs and Psychotropic Substances Act, 1985 ('NDPS Act'). The Sessions Judge had acquitted the Accused by recording a finding that the case of prosecution was not free from doubt and there were many infirmities to hold that the Accused was found to be in possession of charas. High Court in appeal by reappreciating the evidence on record concluded that the prosecution had proved its case beyond reasonable doubt and also has proved that 13 Kg. of charas was recovered from the possession of the Appellant-Accused, who was managing the dhaba in question, and set aside the judgment of the trial court and ordered conviction of the Appellant. Hence, the present appeal. Appellant contended that the well-considered judgment of the trial court was reversed by the High Court without recording cogent reasons.

Held, while partly allowing the Appeal:

i. The trial court acquitted the Appellant mainly on the ground that prosecution case was not supported by independent witnesses; conscious possession was not proved; non-compliance of Section 50 of the NDPS Act; proper procedure was not followed in sending the samples for examination and the case of the prosecution was unnatural and improbable. As rightly held by the High Court, Section 50 of the NDPS Act is applicable only in the case of personal search, as such, there is no basis for the findings recorded by the trial court that there was non-compliance of provision under Section 50 of the NDPS Act. Even with regard to the finding of the trial court that the case of the prosecution was not supported by independent witnesses, it is clear from the evidence on record that the incident had happened at about 10:30 p.m. in a dhaba which is away from the village site and all other persons who are found in the dhaba were the servants of the Accused. It is also clear from the evidence on record that witnesses examined on behalf of the Appellant are closely related to the Accused, as such, they could not be said to be independent witnesses. Another witness was the servant of the dhaba, who cannot be expected to be a witness against his own master.

ii. The view taken by the trial court was not at all possible, having regard to the evidence on record and findings which are erroneously recorded contrary to evidence on record were rightly set aside by the High Court.

iii. The judgment of the High Court does not suffer from any infirmity so as to interfere with the judgment of conviction.

iv. Having regard to peculiar facts and circumstances of the case and in view of the fact that the incident occurred in the year 2001 and as the Appellant claimed to be a priest in the temple, who is now aged about 65 years, we deem it appropriate that it is a fit case to modify the sentence imposed on the Appellant. Accordingly, the sentence awarded on the Appellant is reduced to a period of 10 (ten) years, while maintaining the conviction and the penalty as imposed by the High Court. The appeal was partly allowed to the extent indicated above.

CHAPTER FOUR

MUKESH SINGH VS. STATE (NARCOTIC BRANCH OF DELHI), 2020

Hon'ble Judges/Coram:

Arun Mishra, Indira Banerjee, Vineet Saran, M.R. Shah and S. Ravindra Bhat, JJ.

Equivalent Citation: 2021(2)ACR1982, 2020(214)AIC57, AIR2020SC4794, 2020 (113) ACC 644, 2020 (3) ALT (Crl.) 176 (A.P.), 2020(4)Crimes206(SC), 2020(3)J.L.J.R.429, 2020(4)JKJ133[SC], 2020 (5) KHC 1, 2020-2-LW(Crl)859, 2020(3)MLJ(Crl)674, 2020(3)PLJR379, 2020(3)RCR(Criminal)595, 2020(3)RLW2354(SC), (2020)10SCC120, MANU/SC/0660/2020

Relevant Section/provisions: Sections 41, 42, 43, 44, 53, 53(2) and 58 of Narcotic Drugs and Psychotropic Substances Act, 1985

Number of Pages in the Original Judgment: 28

Ratio Decidendi:

Merely because the informant is the investigator, by that itself the investigation would not suffer the vice of unfairness or bias and therefore on the sole ground that informant is the investigator, the Accused is not entitled to acquittal.

Case Note:

Criminal - Informant as investigator - Validity of investigation - Sections 41, 42, 43, 44, 53, 53(2) and 58 of Narcotic Drugs and Psychotropic

Substances Act, 1985 - This court in case of Mohan Lal v. State of Punjab taking view that in case investigation is conducted by police officer who himself is complainant, trial is vitiated and Accused is entitled to acquittal - Decision of this court in case of Mohan Lal v. State of Punjab came up for consideration subsequently before this Court in case of Varinder Kumar v. State of Himachal Pradesh and three Judge Bench of this Court held that decision of this Court in case of Mohan Lal shall be applicable prospectively - Thus, matter was referred to larger Bench consisting of three Judges - Three Judge Bench had referred to larger Bench of five Judges to consider matter - Hence, present reference - Whether in case investigation was conducted by informant/police officer who himself was complainant, trial was vitiated and in such situation, Accused was entitled to acquittal.

Brief Facts:

Having doubted the correctness of the decision of this Court in the case of Mohan Lal v. State of Punjab taking the view that in case the investigation is conducted by the police officer who himself is the complainant, the trial is vitiated and the Accused is entitled to acquittal, initially by order the matter was referred to a larger Bench consisting of three Judges. A three Judge Bench had referred to a larger Bench of five Judges to consider the matter.

Held, while answering the reference:

i. Section 53 of the NDPS Act provides that the Central Government, after consultation with the State Government, may, by notification published in the Official Gazette, invest any officer of the department of central excise, narcotics, customs, revenue intelligence or any other department of the Central Government including para-military forces or armed forces or any class of such officers with the powers of an officer in charge of a police station for the investigation of the offences under the NDPS Act. Sub-section 2 of Section 53 further provides that the State Government, may, by notification published in the Official Gazette, invest any officer of the department of drugs control, revenue or excise or any other department or any class of such officers with the powers of an officer in charge of a police station for the investigation of offences under the NDPS Act. Therefore, other persons authorised by the Central Government or the State Government can be the officer in charge of a police station for the investigation of the offences. Section 53 does not speak that all those officers to be authorised to exercise the powers of an officer in charge of a police station for the investigation of the offences under the NDPS Act shall be other than those officers authorised under Sections 41, 42, 43, and 44 of the NDPS Act. It appears that the legislature in its wisdom has never thought that the officers authorised to exercise the powers under Sections 41, 42, 43 and 44 cannot be the officer in charge of a police station for the investigation of the offences under the NDPS Act.

ii. Investigation includes even search and seizure. As the investigation is to be carried out by the officer in charge of a police station and none other and therefore purposely Section 53 authorises the Central Government or the State Government, as the case may be, invest any officer of the department of drugs control, revenue or excise or any other department or any class of such officers with the powers of an officer in charge of a police station for the investigation of offences under the NDPS Act.

iii. Section 42 confers power of entry, search, seizure and arrest without warrant or authorisation to any such officer as mentioned in Section 42 including any such officer of the revenue, drugs control, excise, police or any other department of a State Government or the Central Government, as the case may be, and as observed hereinabove, Section 53 authorises the Central Government to invest any officer of the department of central excise, narcotics, customs, revenue intelligence or any other department of the Central Government or any class of such officers with the powers of an officer in charge of a police station for the investigation. Similar powers are with the State Government. The only change in Sections 42 and 53 was that in Section 42 the word police was there, however in Section 53 the word police was not there. There was an obvious reason as for police such requirement was not warranted as he always could be the officer in charge of a police station as per the definition of an officer in charge of a police station as defined under the Code of Criminal Procedure. The NDPS Act did not specifically bar the informant/complainant to be an investigator and officer in charge of a police station for the investigation of the offences under the NDPS Act. On the contrary, it permits. To take a contrary view would be amending Section 53 and the relevant provisions of the NDPS Act and/or adding something which was not there, which was not permissible.

iv. There was no reason to doubt the credibility of the informant and doubt the entire case of the prosecution solely on the ground that the informant has investigated the case. Solely on the basis of some apprehension or the doubts, the entire prosecution version could not be discarded and the Accused was not to be straightway acquitted unless and until the Accused was able to establish and prove the bias and the prejudice. As held by this Court in the case of Ram Chandra (supra) the question of prejudice or bias has to be established and not inferred. The question of bias would have to be decided on the facts of each case. NDPS Act was a Special Act with the special purpose and with special provisions including Section 68 which provides that no officer acting in exercise of powers vested in him under any provision of the NDPS Act or any Rule or order made thereunder shall be compelled to say from where he got any information as to the commission of any offence. Therefore, considering the NDPS Act being a special Act with special procedure to be followed under Chapter V, there was no specific bar against conducting the investigation by the informant himself and in view of the safeguard provided under the Act itself, namely, Section 58, this court was of the opinion that there could not be any general proposition of law to be laid down that in every case where the informant was the investigator, the trial is vitiated and the Accused was entitled to acquittal. Similarly, even with respect to offences under the Indian Penal Code, there was no specific bar against the informant/ complainant investigating the case. Only in a case where the Accused had been able to establish and prove the bias and/or unfair investigation by the informant-cum-investigator and the case of the prosecution was merely based upon the deposition of the informant-cum-investigator, meaning thereby prosecution did not rely upon other witnesses, more particularly the independent witnesses, in that case, where the complainant himself had conducted the investigation, such aspect of the matter can certainly be given due weightage while assessing the evidence on record. Therefore, as rightly observed by this Court in the case of Bhaskar Ramappa Madar, the matter had to be decided on a case to case basis without any universal generalisation. As rightly held by this Court in the case of V. Jayapaul, there was no bar against the informant police officer to investigate the case. As rightly observed, if at all, such investigation could only be assailed on the ground of bias or real likelihood of bias on the part of the investigating officer the question of bias would depend on the facts and circumstances of each case and therefore it was not proper to lay down a broad and unqualified proposition that in every case where the police officer who registered the case by lodging the first information, conducts the investigation that itself had caused prejudice to the Accused and thereby it vitiates the entire prosecution case and the Accused was entitled to acquittal.

CHAPTER FIVE

RIZWAN KHAN VS. THE STATE OF CHHATTISGARH, 2020

Hon'ble Judges/Coram:

Ashok Bhushan, R. Subhash Reddy and M.R. Shah, JJ.

Equivalent Citation: 2020(215)AIC28, AIR2020SC4297, 2020 (2) ALD(Crl.) 1019 (SC), 2021 (116) ACC 301, 2020(5)BLJ505, 2020(4)BomCR(Cri)192, 2020CriLJ4386, 2020(3)Crimes441(SC), 2020(5)JKJ185[SC], 2020(4)RCR(Criminal)114, 2020(4)RLW3315(SC), (2020)9SCC627, 2020 (7-8) SCJ 582, MANU/SC/0680/2020

Relevant Section/provisions: Sections 20(b)(ii)(B), 42 and 55 of Narcotic Drugs and Psychotropic Substances Act, 1985

Number of Pages in the Original Judgment: 08

Case Note:

Criminal - Conviction - Contraband substance - Sections 20(b)(ii)(B), 42 and 55 of Narcotic Drugs & Psychotropic Substances Act, 1985 - Appellant -Accused No. 1 and one another were charged for offence under Section 20(b)(ii)(B) of Act, having in their possession prohibited Narcotic Substance-Ganja - Special Judge held Accused guilty for offence under Section 20(b)(ii)(B) of Act - Feeling aggrieved and dissatisfied with impugned judgment and order of conviction, Appellant preferred appeal before High Court - High Court had dismissed the said appeal preferred by Accused No. 1 and had confirmed the judgment and order of conviction and sentence passed by Special Judge - Hence, present appeal - Whether there was any reason to interfere with conviction of Accused for offence under

Section 20(b)(ii)(B) of NDPS Act.

Brief Facts:

The Appellant - Accused No. 1 and one another were charged for the offence under Section 20(b)(ii)(B) of the NDPS Act, having in their possession prohibited Narcotic Substance-Ganja. On completion of the investigation against the Accused under the NDPS Act, Appellant and one another were chargesheeted for the offence under Section 20(b)(ii)(B) of the NDPS Act and another co-Accused was charged for the offence under Section 20(b)(ii)(C) of the NDPS Act. The Special Judge held the Accused guilty for the offence under Section 20(b)(ii)(B) of the NDPS Act. Feeling aggrieved and dissatisfied with the impugned judgment and order of conviction and sentence passed by the Special Judge, the Appellant preferred an appeal before the High Court. Before the High Court, one of the main submissions on behalf of the Appellant was that as police official who seized the articles and lodged FIR also participated in investigation and therefore the complainant and the investigator being the same, in view of the decision of this Court in the case of Mohan Lal v. State of Punjab, the Accused was entitled to acquittal. The High Court had dismissed the said appeal preferred by Accused No. 1 and had confirmed the judgment and order of conviction and sentence passed by the Special Judge. Hence, the present appeal.

Held, while dismissing the appeal:

i. The prosecution had been successful in proving the case against the Accused by examining the witnesses. It was true that all the witnesses were police officials and two independent witnesses who were panchnama witnesses had turned hostile. However, all the police witnesses were found to be reliable and trustworthy. All of them had been thoroughly cross-examined by the defence. There was no allegation of any enmity between the police witnesses and the Accused. No such defence had been taken in the statement under Section 313, Code of Criminal Procedure. There was no law that the evidence of police officials, unless supported by independent evidence, was to be discarded and/or unworthy of acceptance.
ii. So far as the submission on behalf of the Accused with respect to non-compliance of the procedure prescribed under Section 42 of the NDPS Act was concerned, on considering the deposition of prosecution

witness, compliance of the procedure prescribed under Section 42 of the NDPS Act had been established and proved.

iii. Similarly, compliance under Section 55 of the NDPS Act had also been established and proved by the prosecution by examining prosecution witnesses.

iv. It had been established and proved that the samples which were seized and sealed were sent to the FSL. From the record, it establishes that the recovery from Appellant was marked as B1 and B2 and the treasury record also that the narcotic substances recovered from Rizwan Khan were shown as B1 and B2. There seems to be some clerical error in numbering of sample in memorandum of Superintendent of Police and the same was mentioned as A1. However, it had been established and proved that the samples which were seized and sealed from Appellant were sent to the FSL.

v. To prove the case under the NDPS Act, the ownership of the vehicle is not required to be established and proved. It was enough to establish and prove that the contraband articles were found from the Accused from the vehicle purchased by the Accused. Ownership of the vehicle was immaterial. What was required to be established and proved was the recovery of the contraband articles and the commission of an offence under the NDPS Act. Therefore, merely because of the ownership of the vehicle was not established and proved and/or the vehicle was not recovered subsequently, trial was not vitiated, while the prosecution had been successful in proving and establishing the recovery of the contraband articles from the Accused on the spot.

vi. Both the courts below had rightly convicted the Accused for the offence under Section 20(b)(ii)(B) of the NDPS Act. There was no reason to interfere with the conviction of the Accused for the offence under Section 20(b)(ii)(B) of the NDPS Act.

CHAPTER SIX

KRISHNA PRASAD VERMA (D) THR. L.RS. VS. STATE OF BIHAR AND ORS., 2019

Hon'ble Judges/Coram:

Deepak Gupta and Aniruddha Bose, JJ.

Equivalent Citation: AIR2019SC4852, 2020(1)ALT224, 2020ALT (Rev.) 26, 2020(I)CLR(SC)64, 2019(4)ESC952(SC), 2019 (5) KHC 125, 2019(4)KLT173, 2020LabIC173, 2020(2)MhLj296, 2020(1)MPLJ511, 2019(14)SCALE252, (2019)10SCC640, (2020)1SCC(LS)33, 2021 (1) SCJ 689, 2020(1)SLJ224(SC), 2020(2)SLR613(SC), MANU/SC/1364/2019

Relevant Section/provisions: Article 235 of the Constitution of India, Sections 22, 23 and 24 of the Narcotic Drugs and Psychotropic Substances Act

Number of Pages in the Original Judgment: 07

Ratio Decidendi:

Unless there are clear-cut allegations of misconduct, extraneous influences, gratification of any kind etc., disciplinary proceedings should not be initiated merely on the basis that a wrong order has been passed by the judicial officer or merely on the ground that the judicial order is incorrect.

Case Note:

Service - Disciplinary proceedings - Validity of charges - Present appeal filed against disciplinary action taken by High Court against Appellant-

Judicial Officer on two charges - First charge that Appellant granted bail in one case notwithstanding fact that bail petitions of accused was earlier rejected by High Court - Second charge was Appellant with intent to acquit Accused in narcotics case closed proceeding in great haste resulting in acquittal of accused - Whether disciplinary proceedings initiated against Appellant on alleged charges was sustainable.

Brief Facts:

The High Court initiated disciplinary proceedings on charges that Appellant granted bail to accused in one case notwithstanding the fact that the bail petitions of accused was earlier rejected by High Court. The other charge was that Appellant with an intent to acquit accused in Narcotic case closed the proceeding in great haste resulting in acquittal of accused.

Held, while allowing the appeal:

i. As far as the first charge was concerned, a major fact, which was not considered by the enquiry officer, the disciplinary authority as well as the High Court was that the Additional Public Prosecutor, who had appeared on behalf of the State had not opposed the prayer of the Accused for grant of bail. In case, the public prosecutor did not oppose the bail, then normally any Judge would grant bail.

ii. The main ground to hold the Appellant guilty of the first charge was that the Appellant did not take notice of the orders of the High Court whereby the High Court had rejected the bail application of one of the Accused. It would be pertinent to mention that the High Court itself observed that after framing of charges, if the non-official witnesses were not examined, the prayer for bail could be removed, but after moving the Lower Court first. The officer may had been guilty of negligence in the sense that he did not carefully go through the case file and did not take notice of the order of the High Court which was on his file. This negligence could not be treated to be misconduct. It would be pertinent to mention that the enquiry officer had not found that there was any extraneous reason for granting bail. The enquiry officer virtually sat as a court of appeal picking holes in the order granting bail.

iii. It would be important to mention that it seems that later it was brought to the notice of the Appellant that he had not taken note of the order of the High Court while granting bail. Thereafter, he issued notice to all the three Accused i.e. within less than two months and cancelled the bail granted to all the three Accused. If he had made the mistake of not seeing the whole file, on that being brought to his notice, he corrected the mistake. After the Appellant cancelled the bail and the Accused were again arrested, they again applied for bail and this bail application was rejected by the Appellant.

iv. Coming to the second charge, which is under the Narcotic Drugs and Psychotropic Substances Act, 1985. The Appellant, a Special Judge, closed the evidence of the prosecution which resulted in material witnesses not being examined and consequently the Accused was acquitted. As far as this allegation was concerned, the enquiry officer on the basis of the statements of two clerks of the Court had made lengthy observations that the Appellant did not send any communication to the Superintendent of Police, the District Magistrate and other authorities to ensure the production of the witnesses. According to the enquiry officer, this being a serious matter, the evidence should not have been closed and the Appellant should have made efforts to approach the senior officials to get the witnesses produced. The Code of Criminal Procedure or the NDPS Act did not provide for any such procedure. It was the duty of the prosecution to produce the witnesses. Even in this case, interestingly, the Public Prosecutor had made a note on the side of the daily order-sheet that he was unable to produce the witnesses so the evidences may be closed. Fail to understand how the Appellant had been hanged whereas no action had been taken or recommended against the Public Prosecutor concerned. The enquiry officer, while conducting the enquiry, had noted, while considering the arguments of the delinquent official, that he had raised a plea that he closed the evidence because the Public Prosecutor had made the statement, but while holding the Appellant guilty of misconduct no reference had been made to the statement of the Public Prosecutor.

v. The case of the Appellant was that he had given eighteen adjournments for production of the witnesses to the prosecution in the NDPS case. Such a judicial officer was between the devil and the deep sea. If he keeps on granting adjournments then the High Court would take action against him on the ground that he did not dispose of his cases efficiently and if he closes the evidence then the High Court would take action on the ground that he has let the Accused go scot-free. That is not the purpose of Article 235 of the Constitution of India. That was why this court again repeat that one of the responsibilities of the High Court on the administrative side was to ensure that the independence of the District judiciary was maintained and the High Court acts as a guardian and protector of the District judiciary.

CHAPTER SEVEN

MOHAMMED FASRIN VS. STATE, 2019

Hon'ble Judges/Coram:

Deepak Gupta and Aniruddha Bose, JJ.

Equivalent Citation: 2020(208)AIC148, AIR2019SC4427, 2020 (2) ALD(Crl.) 603 (SC), 2020 (111) ACC 619, 2019 (3) ALT (Crl.) 320 (A.P.), 2019(4)Crimes3(SC), 2019(4)J.L.J.R.85, 2019(4)JCC3968, 2019(5)JKJ43[SC], 2020(4)JKJ479[SC], 2020-2-LW(Crl)456, 2020(1)N.C.C.137, 2019(4)PLJR3, 2019(4)RCR(Criminal)362, (2019)8SCC811, 2020 (1) SCJ 187, MANU/SC/1267/2019

Relevant Section/provisions: Sections 8(c), 21, 23(c), 27(A) and 29 of Narcotic Drugs and Psychotropic Substances Act, 1985

Number of Pages in the Original Judgment: 04

Case Note:

Narcotics - Acquittal - Lack of evidence - Sections 8(c),21,23(c),27(A) and 29 of Narcotic Drugs and Psychotropic Substances Act, 1985 - District and Sessions Judge convicted Accused along with three others for having committed offences related with contraband substance under NDPS Act - Appellant was convicted for having committed offences under Section 8(c) read with 29, 21 and 23(c) and 27(A) of Act and apart from that Appellant had committed offence punishable under Section 8(c) read with 27(A) of Act - High Court, on appeal, upheld conviction passed by Trial Court - Hence, present appeal - Whether Courts below erred in convicting Appellant for alleged offences.

Brief Facts:

The District and Sessions Judge convicted the Accused along with three others for having committed offences under the NDPS Act. As far as the

Appellant WAs concerned, he was convicted for having committed offences under Section 8(c) read with 29, 21 and 23(c) and 27(A) of the NDPS Act and apart from that Appellant had committed the offence punishable under Section 8(c) read with 27(A) of the Act. On appeal, the High Court upheld conviction awarded by Trial Court.

Held, while allowing the appeal:

i. The confessional statement of the Appellant recorded. This Court proceed on the premise that the confession was admissible. Even if it was admissible, the Court had to be satisfied that it was a voluntary statement, free from any pressure and also that the Accused was apprised of his rights before recording the confession. No such material had been brought on the record of this case. The confession of the co-Accused, which was said to be a corroborative piece of evidence, was of no material value. Therefore, other than the two confessional statements - one of the co-Accused and the other of the Accused, the prosecution had gathered no evidence to link the Appellant with the commission of the offence. As such, without going into the legality of the admissibility of the confession, even if these confessions were admissible then also the evidence was not sufficient to convict the Accused.

Both the Trial Court and the High Court wrongly convicted the Accused. Therefore set aside the judgment of both the Courts below

CHAPTER EIGHT

UNION OF INDIA (UOI) VS. LEEN MARTIN AND ORS., 2018

Hon'ble Judges/Coram:

N.V. Ramana and S. Abdul Nazeer, JJ.

Equivalent Citation: 2018(185)AIC232, AIR2018SC991, 2018 (103) ACC 649, 2018ALLMR(Cri)1361, 2018 (1) ALT (Crl.) 394 (A.P.), IV(2018)CCR557(SC), 2019CriLJ928, 2018(1)Crimes128(SC), 2018(1)ECrN 553, 2018(2)JCC102, 2018(3)JKJ181[SC], 2018(2)MLJ(Crl)469, 2018(2)RCR(Criminal)122, 2018(3)RLW2086(SC), 2018(2)SCALE446, (2018)4SCC490, 2018 (5) SCJ 542, 2018(1)UC469, MANU/SC/0141/2018

Relevant Section/provisions: Section 20(b)(ii)(c) and, 28, 23 and 67 of Narcotic Drugs and Psychotropic Substances Act, 1985

Number of Pages in the Original Judgment: 04

Case Note:

Narcotics - Acquittal - Lack of Evidence - Present appeal filed challenging order wherein High Court acquitted first Respondent holding evidence relied by Trial Court as highly inconsistent and full of contradictions - Whether order of acquittal by High Court justifiable

Brief Facts:

The officers of Customs, Air Intelligence Unit, noticed that first Respondent was found to be suspiciously loitering near the airline counters. After completing his immigration and custom formalities, first Respondent was intercepted and subjected to examination by a sniffer dog. When there was an indication about the presence of narcotic or psychotropic substance, he was taken to a baggage examination area. During examination three rectangular packets were discovered containing brown colored substance which tested positive a contraband substance. After completion of the investigation, charges leveled, the Trial Court convicted the first Respondent. An appeal was preferred wherein the High Court acquitted the first Respondent holding that the prosecution failed in establishing that the panchas were present during the seizure procedure and the evidence relied by the Trial Court was highly inconsistent and full of contradictions. Hence, present appeal was filed.

Held, while dismissing the appeal:

i. The present Court found that the evidences were contradicting the statement of the Intelligence Officer. Except the statement made by the first Respondent there was no other material to substantiate the case against the Respondent. The witnesses had categorically stated that, when they were called by the Intelligence Officer, the bag was already opened. Further the panchanama was not read over to them. They were asked to sign on number of papers and they were not aware of the contents. Moreover, the intelligence officer did not state that the bag containing the narcotic substance was opened in the presence of panchas.
ii. The prosecution hinges on the alleged recovery of the narcotic substance from first Respondent but, this very fact was not proved beyond reasonable doubt as independent witnesses had portrayed a different story as to the recovery and seizure.

CHAPTER NINE

MOHAN LAL VS.THE STATE OF PUNJAB, 2018

Hon'ble Judges/Coram:

Ranjan Gogoi, R. Banumathi and Navin Sinha, JJ.

Equivalent Citation: 2018(189)AIC26, AIR2018SC3853, 2019 (1) ALD(Crl.) 696 (SC), 2018 (104) ACC 977, 2018(4)BLJ215, 2018(4)BomCR(Cri)644, IV(2018)CCR543(SC), 2019CriLJ420, 2018(3)Crimes218(SC), 2018(3)J.L.J.R.393, 2018(4)JCC228, 2018(3)JKJ3[SC], 2018 (4) KHC 387, 2018(3)KLT852, 2018-2-LW(Crl)596, 2018(4)MLJ(Crl)244, 2018(3)N.C.C.220, 2018(II)OLR485, 2018(3)PLJR419, (2018)192PLR450, 2018(4)RCR(Criminal)101, 2018(9)SCALE663, 2018 (10) SCJ 540, 2018(3)UC1611, MANU/SC/0857/2018

Relevant Section/provisions: Section of 18 of Narcotic Drugs and Psychotropic Substances Act, 1985

Number of Pages in the Original Judgment: 09

Case Note:

Narcotics - Acquittal - Defective investigation - Section 18 of Narcotic Drugs and Psychotropic Substances Act, 1985 - Present appeal filed against judgment by which Appellant was convicted for offence under Section 18 of Act - Whether in criminal prosecution, it would be in consonance with principles of justice, fair play and fair investigation, if informant and investigating officer were to be same person.

Brief Facts:

An F.I.R. was lodged by informant, that while on patrol duty, he was accompanied by two persons. The witness entertained doubts about the Appellant upon seeing him. A gazetted officer, was called and the Appellant was searched, leading to recovery of opium in a bag carried by him. Upon conclusion of investigation, the Appellant was charge-sheeted, put on trial, and convicted under Section 18 of Act.

Held, while allowing the appeal:

i. In a criminal prosecution, there is an obligation cast on the investigator not only to be fair, judicious and just during investigation, but also that the investigation on the very face of it must appear to be so, eschewing any conduct or impression which may give rise to a real and genuine apprehension in the mind of an Accused and not mere fanciful, that the investigation was not fair. In the circumstances, if an informant police official in a criminal prosecution, especially when carrying a reverse burden of proof, makes the allegations, was himself asked to investigate, serious doubts will naturally arise with regard to his fairness and impartiality. It was not necessary that bias must actually be proved. It would be illogical to presume and contrary to normal human conduct, that he would himself at the end of the investigation submit a closure report to conclude false implication with all its attendant consequences for the complainant himself. The result of the investigation would therefore be a foregone conclusion.

The importance of a fair investigation from the point of view of an Accused as a guaranteed constitutional right under Article 21 of the Constitution of India, it is considered necessary that the law in this regard be laid down with certainty. To leave the matter for being determined on the individual facts of a case, may not only lead to a possible abuse of powers, but more importantly would leave the police, the Accused, the lawyer and the courts in a state of uncertainty and confusion which had to be avoided. It was therefore held that a fair investigation, which was but the very foundation of fair trial, necessarily postulates that the informant and the investigator must not be the same person. Justice must not only be done, but must appear to be done also. Any possibility of bias or a predetermined conclusion had to be excluded. This requirement is all the more imperative in laws carrying a reverse burden of proof. Therefore, the prosecution was held to be vitiated because of the infraction of the constitutional guarantee of a fair investigation.

CHAPTER TEN

SATPAL SINGH VS. THE STATE OF PUNJAB, 2018

Hon'ble Judges/Coram:

Kurian Joseph, Mohan M. Shantanagoudar and Navin Sinha, JJ.

Equivalent Citation: 2018(2)ACR1727, 2018(187)AIC33, AIR2018SC2011, 2018 (104) ACC 307, 2018(2)CGLJ218, 2018CriLJ2843, 2018(3)Crimes81(SC), 2018(3)ECrN 720, 2018(360)ELT791(S.C.), 2018(3)JCC179, 2018(2)JKJ150[SC], 2018-2-LW(Crl)137, 2018(I)OLR876, 2018(4)RLW3206(SC), 2018(5)SCALE519, (2018)13SCC813, 2018 (7) SCJ 12, MANU/SC/0413/2018

Relevant Section/provisions: Sections 438 or 439 of Code of Criminal Procedure, 1973; Sections 22, 29, and 37 of Narcotic Drugs and Psychotropic Substances Act, 1985

Number of Pages in the Original Judgment: 06

Case Note:

Criminal - Anticipatory Bail - Rejection - Sections 438 or 439 of Code of Criminal Procedure, 1973 - Sections 22, 29, and 37 of Narcotic Drugs and Psychotropic Substances Act, 1985 (NDPS Act) - Present appeal filed against order whereby High Court rejected Appellants application of grant of anticipatory bail - Whether order of High Court justifiable

Brief Facts:

The Appellant was an accused under Sections 22 and 29 of the NDPS Act. The High Court had rejected his application for grant of anticipatory bail while had granted anticipatory bail to the co-accused, who are brothers of the Appellant. The Respondent challenged the bail granted to other co-accused while the Appellant filed the present appeal.

Held, while disposing off appeal:

i. The protection under Section 438, Code of Criminal Procedure is available to the accused only till the Court summons the accused based on the charge sheet. On such appearance, the accused had to seek regular bail under Section 439 Code of Criminal Procedure and that application had to be considered by the Court on its own merits. Merely because an Accused was under the protection of anticipatory bail granted under Section 438 Code of Criminal Procedure did not mean that he is automatically entitled to regular bail under Section 439 Code of Criminal Procedure. The satisfaction of the Court for granting protection under Section 438 Code of Criminal Procedure is different from the one under Section 439 Code of Criminal Procedure while considering regular bail.

ii. The order passed by the High Court did not show that there is any reference to Section 37 of the NDPS Act. The quantity is reportedly commercial. In the facts and circumstances of the case, the High Court should not have passed the order under Sections 438 or 439 Code of Criminal Procedure without reference to Section 37 of the NDPS Act and without entering a finding on the required level of satisfaction in case the Court was otherwise inclined to grant the bail.

CHAPTER ELEVEN

MOHINDER SINGH VS. THE STATE OF PUNJAB, 2018

Hon'ble Judges/Coram:

Ranjan Gogoi, R. Banumathi and Navin Sinha, JJ.

Equivalent Citation: 2018(3)ACR2535, 2018(191)AIC222, AIR2018SC3798, 2019 (1) ALD(Crl.) 644 (SC), 2018 (105) ACC 648, 2018 (3) ALT (Crl.) 186 (A.P.), 2018(4)BLJ53, 2018(4)BomCR(Cri)654, 2018CriLJ4213, 2018(3)Crimes227(SC), 2018(II)ILR-CUT355, ILR2018(3)Kerala693, 2018(3)J.L.J.R.440, 2018(4)JCC205, 2019-1-LW(Crl)929, 2018(3)MLJ(Crl)748, 2018(3)N.C.C.252, 2018(4)PLJR29, 2018(4)RCR(Criminal)62, 2019(1)RLW311(SC), 2018(9)SCALE647, 2019 (3) SCJ 191, 2018(3)UC1645, MANU/SC/0863/2018

Relevant Section/provisions: Sections 18 and 50 of Narcotic Drugs and Psychotropic Substances Act, 1985

Number of Pages in the Original Judgment: 05

Case Note:

i. Narcotics - Acquittal - Contraband substance - Sections 18 and 50 of Narcotic Drugs and Psychotropic Substances Act, 1985 - Trial court acquitted Appellant for offence of possession of contraband substance punishable under Section 18 of Act on ground that there was non-compliance of Section 50 of Act - Trial court further held that evidence regarding production of case property before Magistrate was untrustworthy - On appeal, High Court reversed order of acquittal and convicted Appellant under Section 18 of Act - Hence, present appeal - Whether findings of trial court could be said to be distorted conclusions warranting interference. Facts: The Trial court acquitted Appellant for offence of possession of contraband substance punishable under Section 18 of Act on ground that there was non-compliance of Section 50 of Act. The trial court further held that no order of the Magistrate was proved to show that the case property was produced before the court, was brought in evidence to show that the seal of the sample sent to FSL tallied with the seal of the contraband, and it cannot thus be said that the evidence regarding such production of case property before the Magistrate was trustworthy. On appeal, the High Court reversed order of acquittal and convicted Appellant under Section 18 of Act. Held, while allowing the appeal: (i) For proving the offence under the NDPS Act, it is necessary for the prosecution to establish that the quantity of the contraband goods allegedly seized from the possession of the Accused and the best evidence would be the court records as to the production of the contraband before the Magistrate and deposit of the same before the Malkhana or the document showing destruction of the contraband.

ii. The High Court appears to have gone by the oral evidence of prosecution witnesses that the contraband allegedly seized from the Accused was produced before the Magistrate. When the trial court which was in possession of the case records recorded a finding that there was no order of the Magistrate showing the production of the contraband before the court and acquitted the Accused on that basis, the High Court ought not to have interfered with the said order of acquittal.

iii. The findings of the trial court could not be said to be distorted conclusions warranting interference. Based on the oral evidence of prosecution witnesses, the High Court ought not to have interfered with the order of acquittal and the conviction of the Appellant under Section 18 of the NDPS Act could not be sustained.

Brief Facts:

i. Briefly stated case of the prosecution is that on 30.04.1998, Joginder Singh, SI, Police Station Sadar Ludhiana (PW-2) along with other police officials was checking the vehicles on the bridge of Gill Canal towards the side of village Gill. Meanwhile, at about 7.00-7.30 PM, Appellant

Mohinder Singh came on his scooter No. PB-10B-2413. A signal was given to stop the scooter and the Appellant/Accused stopped his scooter. It was suspected that some contraband substance was being carried in the bag. Appellant/Accused was informed of his right of search before a Gazetted Officer or a Magistrate. Joginder Singh (PW-2) called Gurjit Singh, DSP (PW-4) and the bag carried by the Appellant/Accused was searched in his presence and the substance bag was found to be "*opium*". On weighment, it was found to be 7 kilos and 40 gms. Two samples from the recovered "*opium*", each weighing 20 gms were taken and sealed separately having monogram 'JS' and 'GS' and taken into possession *vide* recovery memo Ext.-PE. Case property along with two samples was deposited with Baldev Singh MHC (PW-5). Next day i.e. on 01.05.1998, the case property as well as the sample parcels were produced before the Area Magistrate who is said to have initialled the case property and the sample parcels. The sample parcels were sent to Forensic Science Laboratory (FSL) and subjected to chemical analysis and the contents were found to be "*opium*" in FSL report *vide* Ext. -P1. After completion of the investigation, charge sheet was filed against Appellant Under Section 18 of the NDPS Act.

ii. To prove the guilt of the Accused, the prosecution has examined Constable Hardev Singh (PW-1), SI Joginder Singh (PW-2), ASI Harbhajan Singh (PW-3), DSP Gurjit Singh (PW-4) and Baldev Singh, MHC (PW-5). The Appellant was examined Under Section 313 Code of Criminal Procedure to explain the incriminating evidence circumstance appearing in the prosecution evidence and he denied all of them.

Held, while allowing the appeal:

i. Considering the case in hand, the findings of the trial court cannot be said to be 'distorted conclusions' warranting interference. Based on the oral evidence of Joginder Singh (PW-2) and Harbhajan Singh (PW-3), the High Court ought not to have interfered with the order of acquittal and the conviction of the Appellant Under Section 18 of the NDPS Act cannot be sustained.

ii. In the result, the conviction of the Appellant Under Section 18 of the NDPS Act and the sentence of imprisonment imposed on him is set aside and this appeal is allowed and the Appellant is acquitted of the charge.

CHAPTER TWELVE

KRISHAN CHAND VS. STATE OF H.P., 2017

Hon'ble Judges/Coram:

Pinaki Chandra Ghose and Rohinton Fali Nariman, JJ.

Equivalent Citation: 2019(197)AIC96, AIR2017SC3751, 2017(4)AJR100, 2017 (2) ALD(Crl.) 602 (SC), 2019 (107) ACC 688, 2017(4)Crimes362(SC), 2017(3)JCC112, 2017(6)SCALE468, (2018)1SCC222, 2018 (8) SCJ 199, MANU/SC/0783/2017

Relevant Section/provisions: Section of 20 of Narcotic Drugs and Psychotropic Substances Act, 1985

Number of Pages in the Original Judgment: 06

Case Note:

Narcotics - Acquittal - Lack of evidence - Section 20 of Narcotic Drugs and Psychotropic Substances, Act, 1985 - Case was registered against Appellant under Section 20 of Act for offence of possession of contraband substance - Special Judge held that prosecution had not been able to prove case beyond reasonable doubt acquitted Accused of charge framed against him - Challenging same, Respondent filed appeal before High Court - Division Bench of High Court allowed appeal and set aside judgment of acquittal passed by trial Court - High Court convicted Accused under Section 20 of Act - Hence, present appeal - Whether High Court committed error in convicting Appellant under Section 20 of Act.

Brief Facts:

The case was registered against Appellant under Section 20 of Act for offence of possession of contraband substance. The prosecution, in order to prove its case, has examined as many as six witnesses. The Accused was also examined under Section 313 Code of Criminal Procedure, 1973. He explained that bag did not belong to him and that no charas was recovered from him. He further stated to be innocent, who was falsely implicated. The Special Judge after hearing the parties and considering the materials placed before it, by way of an elaborate judgment, held that the prosecution had not been able to prove the case beyond reasonable doubt acquitted the Accused of the charge framed against him. Challenging the same, the Respondent filed Criminal Appeal before the High Court. The Division Bench of the High Court, allowed the appeal and set aside the judgment of acquittal passed by the trial Court. The High Court convicted the Accused under Section 20 of the NDPS Act.

Held, while allowing the appeal:

i. The Complainant was not the scribe/author of the various memos including the entries as made in NCB form. It had been stated by prosecution witness that the complainant had prepared the search memo of witnesses, seizure memo, arrest memo, seal of H and NCB form in his own hand. The said version had been contradicted by the Complainant himself.
ii. The High Court failed to appreciate that the harsher was the punishment, the more was the strictness of proof required from the prosecution and that failing to associate independent witnesses at the time of recovery created a dent in the case of prosecution.
iii. As rightly pointed out by the Appellant that the High Court failed to appreciate that in the absence of independent witnesses, the evidence of the police witnesses must be scrutinized with greater care especially when police witnesses contradicted themselves on the issue as to in whose hand writing the seizure memo, the arrest memo, consent memo and the NCB form were written and the evidence adduced by the prosecution was not reliable.
iv. Though, in the present case, the prosecution, in support of its case, had examined the Complainant and prosecution witness who had supported the alleged recovery of charas from the Accused. However, there were material contradictions, as pointed in their statements, which make the prosecution case highly doubtful. The High Court by not taking into account the contradictions in the evidence adduced held that in case there were minor contradictions in the depositions of the witnesses, the same were bound to be ignored and convicted the Appellant.

v. In view of the material contradictions, it was found that the High Court wrongly convicted the Appellant as the evidence adduced by the prosecution was not carefully scrutinized by the High Court. The High Court committed error in convicting and sentencing the Appellant.

CHAPTER THIRTEEN

State of Rajasthan Vs. Jag Raj Singh, 2016

Hon'ble Judges/Coram:

Abhay Manohar Sapre and Ashok Bhushan, JJ.

Equivalent Citation: 2016(3)ACR2869, 2016(165)AIC170, AIR2016SC3041, 2016 (2) ALD(Crl.) 376 (SC), 2016 (96) ACC 539, 2016 (2) ALT (Crl.) 314 (A.P.), 2016(3)BomCR(Cri)402, III(2016)CCR88(SC), 2016CriLJ3336, 2016(3)Crimes328(SC), 2016(3)J.L.J.R.176, 2016(3)JCC153, 2016(4)MLJ(Crl)214, 2016(3)N.C.C.276, 2016(3)PLJR285, 2016(3)RCR(Criminal)539, 2016(6)SCALE32, (2016)11SCC687, 2016(2)UC1332, 2016 (3) WLN 106 (SC), MANU/SC/0704/2016

Relevant Section/provisions: Sections 8, 15, 42(1), 42(2) and 43 of Narcotic Drugs and Psychotropic Substances Act, 1985

Number of Pages in the Original Judgment:12

Case Note:

Narcotics - Acquittal - Mandatory provision - Non-compliance thereof - Sections 8, 15, 42(1), 42(2) and 43 of Narcotic Drugs and Psychotropic Substances Act, 1985 - Special Judge convicted Accused under Section 8/15 of Act, 1985 - However, High Court acquitted Accused from charges after setting aside conviction order - Whether High Court committed error in acquitting Accused - Whether there were sufficient material to support findings of High Court regarding non-compliance of Sections 42(1) and 42(2) - Whether Section 43 was applicable in present case - Whether recovery as claimed by Prosecution was supported from evidence on record and material and samples were properly sealed

Brief Facts:

The Special Judge convicted Accused under Section 8/15 of the Narcotic Drugs and Psychotropic Substances Act, 1985. However, the High Court acquitted the Accused from the charges after setting aside the judgment and conviction order. The acquittal was on the grounds that Section 42(2) was not complied with, no ground of belief as contemplated by the proviso was recorded in the present case and search took place after sun set which violates the provisions of Section 42(2) proviso, not a case of conducting the search at public place suddenly and sealing of material sample was not proper nor the sample of seal was deposited in the stock house. Hence, present appeal.

Held, while dismissing the appeal:

i. Section 42(2) requires that where an officer takes down an information in writing under Sub-section (1) he shall sent a copy thereof to his immediate officer senior. The communication which was sent to Circle Officer was not as per the information recorded. Thus, no error was committed by the High Court in coming to the conclusion that there was breach of Section 42(2).
ii. Section 42(1) indicates that any authorised officer can carry out search between sun rise and sun set without warrant or authorisation. The scheme indicates that in event the search has to be made between sun set and sun rise, the warrant would be necessary unless officer has reasons to believe that a search warrant or authorisation cannot be obtained without affording the opportunity for escape of offender which grounds of his belief has to be recorded. In the present case, there was no case that any ground for belief as contemplated by proviso to Sub-section (1) of Section 42 or Sub-section (2) of Section 42 was ever recorded by Station House Officer who proceeded to carry on search. Station House Officer, in his statement also, had not come with any case that as required by the proviso to Sub-section (1), he recorded his grounds of belief anywhere.
iii. Special Judge coming to compliance of proviso to Section 42(1) held that vehicle searched was being used to transport passengers as had been clearly sated by its owner, hence, as per the explanation to Section 43 of the Act, the vehicle was a public transport vehicle and there was no need of any warrant or authority to search such a vehicle. The High Court reversed the findings of the Special Judge.

iv. Admittedly the vehicle was intercepted and was seized by the police. The vehicle could not be said to be a public conveyance within the meaning of Explanation to Section 43. Hence, Section 43 was clearly not attracted and provisions of Section 42(1) proviso were required to be complied with and the aforesaid statutory mandatory provisions having not been complied with, the High Court did not commit any error in setting aside the conviction.

v. The present was a case where prosecution himself has come with case that secret information was received from informer which information was recorded in Roznamacha and thereafter the Station House Officer with police party proceeded towards the scene. The present was not a case where the Station House Officer suddenly carried out search at a public place. The Station House Officer had also come up with the facts and case to prove compliance of Section 42. When search is conducted after recording information under Section 42(1), the provisions of Section 42 has to be complied with.

vi. The present was not a case where Section 43 can be said to have been attracted, hence, non-compliance of Section 42(1) proviso and Section 42(2) had seriously prejudiced the Accused.

The present was not a case where insofar as compliance of Section 42(1) proviso even an arguments based on substantial compliance is raised there is total non-compliance of Section 42(1) proviso. As observed above, Section 43 being not attracted search was to be conducted after complying the provisions of Section 42. The High Court rightly held that non compliance of Section 42(1) and Section 42(2) were proved on the record and the High Court had not committed any error in setting aside the conviction order.

CHAPTER FOURTEEN

SURINDER KUMAR KHANNA VS. INTELLIGENCE OFFICER DIRECTORATE OF REVENUE INTELLIGENCE, 2018

Hon'ble Judges/Coram:

Abhay Manohar Sapre and U.U. Lalit, JJ.

Equivalent Citation: 2018(189)AIC70, AIR2018SC3574, 2018 (2) ALD(Crl.) 763 (SC), 2018 (104) ACC 959, 2018 (3) ALT (Crl.) 126 (A.P.), 2018(4)BLJ4, 2018(3)BomCR(Cri)585, 2018(3)CLJ(SC)41, 2018CriLJ4346, 2018(3)Crimes464(SC), 2018(3)ECrN 121, 2018(362)ELT935(S.C.), ILR2018(3)Kerala517, 2018(3)J.L.J.R.374, 2018(4)JCC189, 2018(3)JKJ39[SC], 2018(3)KLJ808, 2018(3)KLT1027, 2018(3)MLJ(Crl)753, 2018(3)N.C.C.163, 2018(II)OLR745, 2018(3)PLJR395, 2018(3)RCR(Criminal)954, 2018(9)SCALE328, (2018)8SCC271, 2018 (10) SCJ 430, 2018(3)UC1676, MANU/SC/0796/2018

Relevant Section/provisions: Sections 21(c) and 29 of Narcotic Drugs and Psychotropic Substances Act, 1985

Number of Pages in the Original Judgment: 06

Case Note:

Narcotics - Acquittal - Contraband substance - Sections 21(c) and 29 of Narcotic Drugs and Psychotropic Substances Act, 1985 - Trial Court convicted Appellant for offence of possession of contraband substance punishable under Section 21(c) read with Section 29 of Act - High Court confirmed conviction awarded to Appellant - Hence, present appeal - Whether Appellant entitled to be acquitted from charges leveled against him. Facts: The Trial Court convicted Appellant for offence of possession of contraband substance punishable under Section 21(c) read with Section 29 of Narcotic Drugs and Psychotropic Substances Act, 1985. The High Court confirmed conviction awarded to Appellant. Held, while allowing the appeal: It was accepted that apart from the aforesaid statements of co-accused there is no material suggesting involvement of the Appellant in the crime in question. On the touchstone of law laid down by this Court such a confessional statement of a co-accused could not by itself be taken as a substantive piece of evidence against another co-accused and could at best be used or utilized in order to lend assurance to the Court. In the absence of any substantive evidence it would be inappropriate to base the conviction of the Appellant purely on the statements of co-accused. The Appellant was therefore entitled to be acquitted of the charges leveled against him.

Brief Facts:

i. On a specific information that narcotic drugs were going to be transported from Jammu side to Chandigarh via Hoshiarpur in a white colour Indica car bearing registration No. PB-02AJ-7288, the officers of Directorate of Revenue Intelligence (for short 'DRI') laid picket at toll barrier at Hoshiarpur-Garhshankar road. At 10:35 hours, they intercepted an Indica car of white colour which was coming from Hoshiarpur side bearing registration No. PB-02AJ-7288. The car was being driven by one Raj Kumar @ Raju whereas one Surinder Pal Singh was sitting next to him. To ensure safe search of the car and personal search of occupants, the car was taken to the office of Superintendent, Central Excise Range, Model Town, Hoshiarpur. The officers of DRI served notice Under Section 50 of the NDPS Act upon said Raj Kumar @ Raju and Surinder Pal Singh.

ii. As desired by said suspects, their personal searches and that of the car were conducted in the presence of independent witnesses and Shri SJS Chugh, Senior Intelligence Officer. Personal searches of the suspects did not result in recovery of any incriminating material. However, when the car was searched, four packets wrapped with yellowish adhesive tapes were found concealed in the door of dickey of the car. The gross weight of those four packets came to 4.300 kg.

iii. Each of those packets was containing white colour granules/powder which gave a very pungent smell. The pinch of each packet was tested, which showed the presence of heroin. The recovered heroin weighing 3.990 kgs was valued at Rs. 19,95,000/-. Those four packets were taken into possession. Two representative samples of 5 gms each were taken out from each of the packets as per rules. Indica car was also seized by the officers of DRI. Statements of both the suspects were recorded. From their statements, it transpired that four packets of heroin had been taken from one Mr. Goldy r/o Vijaypur, Jammu and those packets were to be delivered to a person of African origin near PGI Chandigarh.

iv. Initially a complaint Under Sections 21, 22, 23, 28, 29 and 60 of the NDPS Act was lodged against said Raj Kumar @ Raju and Surinder Pal Singh. During investigation, the involvement of the present Appellant in the drug racket was said to have been made out. After the Appellant was arrested, a supplementary complaint was presented against him and the matter was taken up with the main complaint. After hearing arguments, charges were framed against said Raj Kumar @ Raju and Surinder Pal Singh and the Appellant for the offences Under Sections 21, 29 and 60 of the NDPS Act.

Held, while allowing the appeal:

i. The law so laid down has always been followed by this Court except in cases where there is a specific provision in law making such confession of a co-accused admissible against another accused.

In the present case it is accepted that apart from the aforesaid statements of co-accused there is no material suggesting involvement of the Appellant in the crime in question. We are thus left with only one piece of material that is the confessional statements of the co-accused as stated above. On the touchstone of law laid down by this Court such a confessional statement of a co-accused cannot by itself be taken as a substantive piece of evidence against another co-accused and can at best be used or utilized in order to lend assurance to the Court. In the absence of any substantive evidence it would be inappropriate to base the conviction of the Appellant purely on the statements of co-accused. The Appellant is therefore entitled to be acquitted of the charges leveled against him. We, therefore, accept this appeal, set aside the orders of conviction and sentence and acquit the Appellant. The Appellant shall be released forthwith unless his custody is required in connection with any other offence.

CHAPTER FIFTEEN

STATE OF HARYANA VS. ASHA DEVI AND ORS., 2015

Hon'ble Judges/Coram:

Pinaki Chandra Ghose and U.U. Lalit, JJ.

Equivalent Citation: 2015(3)ACR2887(SC), 2015VI AD (S.C.) 449, 2015(151)AIC105, 2015(152)AIC129, AIR2015SC3189, 2015(4)AJR397, 2016 (1) ALD(Crl.) 33 (SC), 2015 (90) ACC 335, 2015 (91) ACC 366, 2015ALLMR(Cri)3266, 2015 (3) ALT (Crl.) 74 (SC), 2015(3)BLJ128, 2015(3)BomCR(Cri)147, II(2015)CCR429(SC), 2015CriLJ3406, 2015(3)Crimes289(SC), 2015(4)Crimes262(SC), 2015(3)JCC123(SC), (2015) 3 MLJ(Crl) 119 (SC), 2016(1)N.C.C.219, 2015(2)RCR(Criminal)1018, 2015(6)SCALE258, (2015)8SCC39, 2015 (6) SCJ 396, 2015(2)UC1165, MANU/SC/0602/2015

Relevant Section/provisions: Sections 20 and 29 of Narcotic Drugs and Psychotropic Substances Act, 1985

Number of Pages in the Original Judgment: 05

Case Note:

Narcotics - Acquittal - Sufficiency of evidence - Sections 20 and 29 Narcotic Drugs and Psychotropic Substances Act, 1985 - High Court declined to grant leave to appeal to State against acquittal of Respondents-Accused - Hence, present appeal - Whether acquittal on grounds that there was no independent witness, 2nd Accused could not have fled in presence of five police officers and tampering of sample, was sustainable - Held, both police official and Investigating Officer deposed that public persons were available when contraband was seized, however, none acceded to their request of joining investigation as independent witness - Courts below have found it unbelievable but no reason for same was rendered - Finding that 2nd Accused could not have fled away was on assumption and conjecture - All persons who possessed contraband sample was brought on record to support that no tampering was done with samples - Movement of sample was proved and found to be regular, Prosecution sufficiently proved its case to establish guilt of Accused - Accused were found guilty under Section 20 of Act for possession of contraband substance - Impugned order set aside - Appeal allowed.

Brief Facts:

The facts of this case, as per the prosecution story, are that on 3.2.2006, when Sub Inspector Ram Phal, ASI Rishi Raj, Constable Surender Singh, Lady Constables Babita Rani and Promila, were on patrol duty in a police vehicle which was being driven by Constable Darshan Singh, near Chimni Bai Dharamshala, NIT No. 3, SI Ram Phal received a secret information that Om Prakash son of Moti Lal, and his wife Asha Devi, residents of Gali No. 1, Jhuggi Kalyanpuri, bring Ganja (intoxicated drug) from Madhya Pradesh and supply in Faridabad and if a raid is conducted at their house, Ganja in heavy quantity would be recovered. On receiving this information, the aforesaid police team raided the house of Om Prakash. On seeing the police party, Om Prakash managed to escape by scaling over the wall of the house. Asha Devi also tried to escape but she was apprehended with the help of Lady Constables. On query she disclosed her name as Asha wife of Om Prakash and also disclosed that the man who had escaped from the house was Om Prakash. A notice in writing Under Section 50 of the Narcotic Drugs and Psychotropic Substances Act, 1985 ("NDPS Act", for short) was served on her informing her of the right to either allow the Sub Inspector to take search of her house or opt for the search in presence of some Gazetted Officer or a Magistrate. Asha Devi consented for search of her house in the presence of some Gazetted Officer. Accordingly, Shri Maharaj Singh, the then Deputy Superintendent of Police, NIT, Faridabad, reached the spot and in his presence the house of Asha Devi was searched. Asha Devi unpacked a box, took out a bag containing Ganja and produced it before the Sub-Inspector. The bag was weighed and found to be contained 11 Kgs. of Ganja out of which two samples of 200 gms. each were taken and sealed with letters "RP" and "MS" on the seal. Both the samples along with the residue and the specimen seal impressions were taken into possession by the police under the recovery memo which was prepared by I.O. Ramphal and witnessed by ASI Tej Ram and ASI Rishiraj and attested by DSP Maharaj Singh and thumb mark of Asha Devi. The case property along with the samples and the witnesses were produced before the Station House Officer, who after verifying the facts affixed his seal thereon and were deposited in the Moharrer Police Malkhana. A case was registered against accused Asha Devi Under Section 20(61) of the NDPS Act and she was arrested. Thereafter, on 04.02.2006 case property and both samples were produced before the learned Judicial Magistrate, 1st Class, Faridabad. The learned judicial Magistrate broke the seals on the case property as well one of the samples. The learned Judicial Magistrate verified the material, photographs were taken and contraband was weighed; thereafter the sample was resealed with the seal of RP. The Judicial Magistrate directed the Investigation Officer to deposit the material to Judicial Malkhana. After investigation, accused Asha Devi was charged Under Section 20 of the NDPS Act and accused Om Prakash was charged Under Sections 28 & 29 of the NDPS Act. The accused pleaded not guilty and hence the case was committed for trial.

Held, while allowing the appeal:

Before sentencing, following the principle laid down in Allauddin Mian (supra), this matter was adjourned, giving a chance to the Respondents/ accused to place facts before us and further directed the Appellant to find out about the conduct of the Respondents after this incident and to inform this Court. On the adjourned date, the learned Counsel for the Appellant and learned Counsel for the Respondents/accused expressed that the Respondents thereafter were not found to be implicated in any other matter. After hearing the learned Counsel for the parties and after giving due weight to the mitigating as well as the aggravating circumstances placed before us, we think that it would be proper for us to convict the accused persons with the sentence passed by us, which would serve the purpose.

Accordingly, we set aside the judgment and order passed by the High Court as also by the Trial Court and direct that the accused/Respondents shall be taken into custody forthwith to undergo the sentence. The appeal is accordingly allowed.

CHAPTER SIXTEEN

STATE OF RAJASTHAN VS. SAHI RAM, 2019

Hon'ble Judges/Coram:

U.U. Lalit and Vineet Saran, JJ.

Equivalent Citation: 2020(208)AIC95, AIR2019SC4723, 2019 (2) ALD(Crl.) 1012 (SC), 2020 (111) ACC 938, 129(2020)CLT171, 2020CriLJ153, 2019(4)JCC4009, 2019(4)JKJ453[SC], 2019(4)MLJ(Crl)231, 2020(I)MPJR(SC)31, 2019(4)RCR(Criminal)685, 2020(1)RLW567(SC), 2019(13)SCALE135, (2019)10SCC649, 2019(3)UC1614, MANU/SC/1342/2019

Relevant Section/provisions: Sections 8 and 15 of Narcotic Drugs and Psychotropic Substances Act, 1985

Number of Pages in the Original Judgment: 08

Case Note:

Narcotics - Conviction - Contraband substance - Sections 8 and 15 of Narcotic Drugs and Psychotropic Substances Act, 1985 - Charge sheet was filed against Respondent and against two persons for offence of possession of contraband substance punishable under Section 8 read with 15 of Act - After considering relevant evidence on record, Special Judge, found that case was established against Respondent and he was convicted for offence punishable under Section 8 read with 15 of Act - On appeal, High Court set aside judgment passed by Special Judge and acquitted Respondent of charge levelled against him - Hence, present appeal - Whether High Court erred in acquitting accused of charge levelled against him.

Brief Facts:

An charge-sheet was filed against the Respondent and against two persons for the offence punishable under Section 8 read with 15 of the

NDPS Act. After considering the relevant evidence on record, the Special Judge, found that the case was established against the Respondent and he was convicted for offence punishable under Section 8 read with 15 of the NDPS Act. On appeal against said judgment, the High Court allowed the appeal, set aside the judgment and Order passed by the Special Judge and acquitted the Respondent of the charge levelled against him.

Held, while allowing the appeal:

i. The evidence of prosecution witness shows that from and out of seven bags of poppy husk, samples were taken out of each bag. The bags were also independently sealed and taken in custody and seizure memo which recorded all these facts was also signed by the Accused. At no stage even a suggestion was put to the witness that either the signatures of the Accused were taken by fraud, coercion or mis-representation or that the signatures were not of the Accused or that they did not understand the purport of the seizure memo. It would therefore be difficult to even suggest that the seizure of contraband was not proved by the prosecution.
ii. If the seizure of the material was otherwise proved on record and was not even doubted or disputed the entire contraband material need not be placed before this Court. If the seizure was otherwise not in doubt, there was no requirement that the entire material ought to be produced before the Court. At times the material could be so bulky, for instance as in the present material when those bags that it may not be possible and feasible to produce the entire bulk before the Court. If the seizure was otherwise proved, what was required to be proved was the fact that the samples taken from and out of the contraband material were kept intact, that when the samples were submitted for forensic examination the seals were intact, that the report of the forensic experts shows the potency, nature and quality of the contraband material and that based on such material, the essential ingredients constituting an offence were made out.

The conclusion drawn by the High Court was completely unsustainable and the High Court erred in extending the benefit of acquittal to the Respondent. Therefore, set aside the view taken by the High Court and restore the order of conviction as recorded by the trial court against the Respondent.

CHAPTER SEVENTEEN

GANGARAM VS. THE STATE OF MADHYA PRADESH, 2019

Hon'ble Judges/Coram:

L. Nageswara Rao and M.R. Shah, JJ.

Equivalent Citation: 2020(205)AIC190, 2020 (110) ACC 262, 2019(4)BLJ250, 2019(3)JCC2042, 2019(2)JKJ244[SC], 2019(2)JLJ503, 2019(2)N.C.C.737, 2019(7)SCALE529, (2019)6SCC244, 2019(2)UC1139, MANU/SC/0668/2019

Relevant Section/provisions: Sections 8 and 15 (c) of Narcotic Drugs and Psychotropic Substances Act, 1985

Number of Pages in the Original Judgment: 06

Case Note:

Narcotics - Conviction - Legality - Sections 8 and 15 (c) of Narcotic Drugs and Psychotropic Substances Act, 1985 (NDPS Act) - Present Appeal was filed against judgment of High Court by which conviction of Appellant under Section 8 read with Section 15 (c) of NDPS Act and sentence of 10 years with fine of Rs. 1 lakh was affirmed by High Court - Whether there was a failure on part of prosecution to prove offence alleged against Appellant - Whether Appellant had been rightly convicted under Section 8 read with Section 15 of NDPS Act.

Brief Facts:

FIR was registered in the police station. The narcotic drug was unloaded from the truck and was found to be 415 kilograms in weight. Each bag was marked as Article 1 to Article 10 and two samples of 250 grams from each bag were taken and sealed. The samples of poppy straw were sent to the Forensic Science Laboratory for chemical examination in which it was found that the seized materials are pieces of poppy straw. On completion of investigation, a charge sheet was filed. The Accused denied committing any offence. Though he made a prayer for summoning 10 witnesses in his defence, he did not adduce any evidence by summoning any witnesses. The defence of the Appellant was that he was legally transporting the goods of the licensee contractor Bishan Singh who had a valid licence issued by the District Excise Officer. A charge was framed against the Appellant under Section 8 read with Section 15 and Section 8 read with Section 26 of the NDPS Act. Trial Court convicted the Appellant under Section 8 read with Section 15 (c) of the NDPS Act and sentenced him to undergo an imprisonment of 10 years and to pay a fine of Rs. 1 lakh. The truck which was seized was held liable for confiscation in accordance with the provisions of Section 60(3) of the NDPS Act. The Trial Court directed confiscation of the vehicle and sale of the same by public auction after the period of appeal expired. The High Court affirmed the conviction and sentence of the Appellant finding no fault was committed by the Trial Court.

Held, while dismissing the appeal:

i. Section 8 of the NDPS Act prohibits cultivation of opium poppy and also prohibits, inter alia, production, manufacture, possession, sale, purchase, and transport of any narcotic drug or psychotropic substance.
ii. Section 26 deals with a wilful breach of a condition of the licence for which a penalty is not prescribed elsewhere in the NDPS Act and prescribes punishment with imprisonment for a term that may extend to three years or with fine or with both. Section 15 of the NDPS Act provides that contravention of a licence for transportation of poppy straw involving commercial quantity shall be punishable with rigorous imprisonment for a term which shall not be less than 10 years but may extend to 20 years and a fine which shall not be less than one lakh rupees which may extend to two lakh rupees.
iii. It is clear from the record that, the Appellant admitted the seizure of 10 bags of poppy straw from a truck which was stationed at village Palasiya. The only defence before the Courts below was that the transportation was legal as it was being done on the strength of a valid licence issued by a competent authority. The truck was standing on a road near village

Palasiya which is 18 kilometers away from one of the villages which is mentioned in the license and from where the Appellant could have loaded and transported the poppy straw according to the licence. The conclusion of the Trial Court regarding the guilt of the Appellant under Section 8 read with Section 15 of the NDPS Act does not call for any interference. Though the Appellant initially informed the Court that he wanted to examine 10 defence witnesses, he did not summon any of them to depose in the Court.

iv. Punishment under Section 26 (d) is for breach of a condition of a licence for which a penalty is not prescribed elsewhere in the Act. Section 15 of the Act deals with punishment for contravention in relation to, amongst other things, transportation of poppy straw. In case the contravention involves commercial quantity, a person shall be sentenced to rigorous imprisonment for not less than 10 years according to Section 15. As the contravention of license in relation to poppy straw has been dealt with in Section 15, Section 26 of the Act is not attracted. Courts below are right in holding that, the Appellant is liable to conviction under Section 8 read with Section 15 of the NDPS Act. Appeal dismissed.

CHAPTER EIGHTEEN

Tara Singh and Ors. Vs. Union of India (UOI) and Ors., 2016

Hon'ble Judges/Coram:

Dipak Misra and S.K. Singh, JJ.

Equivalent Citation: 2016(3)ACR2654, 2016(164)AIC184, AIR2016SC3058, 2016 (2) ALD(Crl.) 356 (SC), 2016 (3) ALT (Crl.) 15 (A.P.), 2016(4)BLJ43, 2016(3)BomCR(Cri)679, III(2016)CCR148(SC), 2016CriLJ4199, 2017(1)Crimes176(SC), 2016(3)J.L.J.R.251, 2016(4)JCC229, 2016(4)MLJ(Crl)205, 2016(3)PLJR360, 2016(3)RCR(Criminal)482, 2016(6)SCALE61, (2016)11SCC335, 2016 (7) SCJ 424, 2016(2)UC1277, MANU/SC/0705/2016

Relevant Section/provisions: Section 42 and 15 of Narcotic Drugs and Psychotropic Substances Act, 1985

Number of Pages in the Original Judgment: 09

Case Note:

Criminal - Grant of remission - Seeking thereof - Writ of mandamus - Sections 21, 32A and 37 of Narcotic Drugs and Psychotropic Substances Act, 1985, Articles 32, 72, 141 and 161 of Constitution of India and Sections 432 and 433A of Code of Criminal Procedure, 1973 - Petitioners were convicted for offence punishable under Section 21 of Act, 1985 - Present petition filed seeking grant of remission to Petitioner as per provisions contained in Chapter XIX of Manual, 1996 - Whether writ of mandamus could be issued to authorities to grant remission to Petitioners

Brief Facts:

The Petitioners were convicted for the offence punishable under Section 21 of the Narcotic Drugs and Psychotropic Substances Act, 1985 and sentenced to undergo rigorous imprisonment for more than 10 years and to pay a fine of Rs. 1 lakh. The present petition filed with prayer for issue of writ of mandamus to the Respondent Nos. 1 to 3 commanding them to grant remission to them as per the provisions contained in Chapter XIX of the New Punjab Jail Manual, 1996.

It was the case of the Petitioners that Chapter XIX of the Manual lays down remission and award to the convicts depending upon good conduct and performance of duties allotted to them while they are undergoing sentence, but the benefit under the Chapter XIX of the Manual was not made available to the convicts under the Act, 1985 on the ground that Section 32A of the Act, 1985 bars entitlement to such remission. It had been contended that the denial of benefit sought for by the Petitioner was absolutely arbitrary.

Held, while dismissing the petition:

i. Chapter XIX of the Manual deals with remission and reward. Paragraphs 563 to 588 deal with remission system. Paragraphs 589 and 590 deal with reward. Paragraph 563 states that remission can be granted to prisoners by the State Government/Inspector-General/Superintendent Jails which is subject to withdrawal/forfeiture/revocation. It is not a right and the State Government reserves the right to debar/withdraw any prisoner or category of prisoners from the concession of remission. Paragraph 565 stipulates that remission is of three types, namely, ordinary remission, special remission and the State Government remission. Paragraph 567 postulates the eligibility criteria for prisoners who will be eligible for earning the State Government remission. Paragraph 571 provides what would constitute non-eligibility to get ordinary remission. Paragraph 572 lays down that ordinary remission is not earnable for certain offences committed after admission to jail. Paragraph 576 deals with remission for good conduct. Paragraph 581 provides for special remission. It lays down that special remission may be given to any prisoner except such prisoners who are deprived of remission by way of punishment whether entitled to ordinary remission or not for special reasons.

ii. Section 432 deals with power to suspend or remit sentences. Section 433 deals with power to commute sentences. Section 433A lays the postulate for restrictions on powers of remission or commutation in certain cases.

iii. Section 433A does not and cannot affect even a wee bit the pardon power of the Governor or the President. The necessary sequel to this logic is that notwithstanding Section 433-A the President and the Governor continue to exercise the power of commutation and release under the aforesaid articles.

iv. The exercise of powers under Article 72 or 161 is quite different than the statutory power of remission. On that fundamental bedrock, the provision enshrined under Section 32A, barring a part of the provision, has been held constitutionally valid in case of Dadu @ Tulsidas v. State of Maharashtra.

v. The Petitioners invoked the power of present Court to grant the benefit of remission in exercise of power under Article 32 of the Constitution of India. The prayer was totally misconceived. It was urged in a different manner that the power exercised by this Court under Article 32 and Article 142 of the Constitution cannot be statutorily controlled. Though the argument struck a note of innovation, yet the innovation in the case at hand cannot be allowed to last long, for it invites immediate repulsion. Section 32A of the Act, 1985 as far as it took away the power of the Court to suspend the sentence awarded to the convict under the Act has been declared unconstitutional in case of Dadu @ Tulsidas v. State of Maharashtra. A convict can pray for suspension of sentence when the appeal is pending for adjudication. Negation of the power of the courts to suspend the sentence which has been declared as unconstitutional, as has been held in Dadu @ Tulsidas v. State of Maharashtra, does not confer a right on the convict to ask for suspension of the sentence as a matter of right in all cases nor does it absolve the courts of their legal obligation to exercise the power of suspension within the parameters prescribed under Section 37 of the Act, 1985. The constitutional power exercised under Articles 72 and 161 is quite different than the power exercised under a statute.

vi. Article 32 of the Constitution of India enables a citizen to move present Court for enforcement of his fundamental rights. Moving present Court for the said purpose is fundamental.

vii. The present factual matrix did not remotely suggest that there has been violation of any fundamental right. There was no violation of any law which affects the fundamental rights of the Petitioners. The argument that when a pardon or remission can be given under Article 72 or 161 of the Constitution by the constitutional authority, this Court can exercise the similar power under Article 32 of the Constitution of India was absolutely based on an erroneous premise. Article 32 can be only invoked when there is violation of any fundamental right or where the Court takes up certain grievance which falls in the realm of public interest litigation.

viii. The argument to invoke Article 142 in conjunction with Article 32 of the Constitution was absolutely fallacious and we unhesitatingly repel the same.

CHAPTER NINETEEN

Myla Venkateswarlu Vs. The State of Andhra Pradesh, 2012

Hon'ble Judges/Coram:

Aftab Alam and Ranjana Prakash Desai, JJ.

Equivalent Citation: 2012(2)ACR1546(SC), 2012(113)AIC111, AIR2012SC1619, 2013(2)AJR607, 2012(1)ALD(Cri)875, 2012 (77) ACC 662, 2013(1)ALT(Cri)385, 2012BomCR(Cri)56, II(2012)CCR126(SC), 2013(1)CGLJ426, 2011(2)CLJ(SC)177, 2012CriLJ2262, 2012MLJ(Crl)675, 2012(1)N.C.C.703, 2012(3)RCR(Criminal)72, RLW2012(2)SC1706, 2012(4)SCALE199, (2012)5SCC226, 2012(2)UC1128, 2012(2)WLN75, MANU/SC/0307/2012

Relevant Section/provisions: Section 8(c), 20(b)(i) and 50(1) of Narcotic Drugs and Psychotropic Substances Act, 1985

Number of Pages in the Original Judgment: 05

Case Note:

Narcotics - Conviction - Legality of - Section 8(c), 20(b)(i) and 50(1) of Narcotic Drugs and Psychotropic Substances Act, 1985 - Appeal against judgment of Single Judge of High Court dismissing Appeal filed by Appellant questioning correctness of judgment of conviction passed by Additional Sessions Judge - Whether there was any violation of procedure contemplated under Section 50 of NDPS Act - Whether there was strict compliance of Section 50(1) of NDPS Act - Held, under provision of Section

50 of NDPS Act, suspect could insist that his search be conducted before a gazetted officer or a Magistrate - A suspect might insist on presence of a gazetted officer or a Magistrate so as to introduce transparency in search - Strict compliance with provisions of Section 50(1) of NDPS Act, was necessary - There was no clear communication to Accused that they had a right to be searched in presence of a gazetted officer or a Magistrate - Concept of substantial compliance could not be read into provisions of Section 50(1) of NDPS Act - Therefore, there was a breach of Section 50(1) of NDPS Act - Conviction of Appellant was solely based on possession of Ganja recovered from him - Thus, it would have to be set aside - Accused 1 and Accused 2 were not in Appeal before this Court - Conclusion drawn by this Court applied to their case as well - In circumstances, impugned order convicting Appellant, Accused 1 and Accused 2, was quashed and set aside - Appellant, Accused 1 and Accused 2, were acquitted of charge under Section 8(c) read with Section 20(b)(i) of NDPS Act - Appeal disposed of

Brief Facts:

i. The challenge in this appeal, by special leave, is to the judgment of a learned Single Judge of the Andhra Pradesh High Court dismissing the criminal appeal filed by the Appellant questioning the correctness of the judgment and order passed by the 1st Additional Sessions Judge, Guntur. By the said judgment, the Appellant (original accused 3) and two others viz. Myla Rambabu and Myla Muralikrishna (original accused 1 and 2 respectively and for convenience, referred to as "A1" and "A2" respectively) were convicted for offences punishable Under Section 8(c) read with Section 20(b) (i) of the Narcotic Drugs and Psychotropic Substances Act, 1985, (for short, "the NDPS Act") and sentenced to undergo rigorous imprisonment for six months each and to pay a fine of Rs. 5,000/- each. In default of payment of fine, they were directed to undergo simple imprisonment for six months each.

ii. According to the prosecution, on 5/1/2001, PW-3 CI Koteswara Rao on receiving reliable information about illegal sale of Ganja at Koneru Bazar, Chenchupeta, Tenali, proceeded to Koneru Bazar along with PW-1 PC Shaik Khasim, PW-2 SI Nageswara Rao and one other constable. They noticed the Appellant, A1 and A2 sitting under a bridge. On seeing them, the Appellant, A1 and A2 tried to run away. PW- 3 CI Koteswara Rao and his team apprehended them. The prosecution story further goes on to say that the Appellant, A1 and A2 revealed their names. On questioning, they stated that they were carrying Ganja packets in their pockets. It is further the case of the prosecution that PW-3 CI Koteswara Rao asked them whether they wanted any other gazetted officer for their search and seizure in addition to him to which they replied that they did not want any other gazetted officer and checking by the Circle Inspector of Police was sufficient. In the search, five Ganja packets were recovered from A1, six Ganja packets were recovered from A2 and four Ganja packets were recovered from the Appellant. A1, A2 and the Appellant are stated to have confessed to the crime. They were then put under arrest. After completion of the investigation, they were charged for the offence Under Sections 8(c) read with Section 20(b)(i) of the Narcotic NDPS. The Appellant pleaded not guilty to the charge. The evidence led by the prosecution found favour with the trial Court and it convicted the Appellant, A1 and A2 as aforesaid. The appeal carried from the said judgment was dismissed by the High Court. Hence, this appeal. It must be noted here that A1 and A2 have not challenged the impugned judgment and order and, hence, they are not before us.

Held, while convicting the accused:

A1 and A2 are not before us. However, the conclusion drawn by us applies to their case as well. This Court in Ashok @ Dangra Jaiswal v. State of Madhya Pradesh MANU/SC/0340/2011 : 2011 (4) SCALE 273 dealt with a somewhat similar fact situation. Out of the three accused convicted Under Sections 8(c) and 20(b)(i) of the NDPS Act, only one accused had appealed to this Court. The other two were in jail. This Court set aside the conviction and sentence of the Appellant therein and observed that the lapses which had weighed with it for setting aside the conviction of the Appellant therein apply equally to the case of the accused who had not appealed and, therefore, it would be unjust to let them rot in jail even while allowing the appeal preferred by the Appellant therein. We are respectfully inclined to follow the same course. In the circumstances, the impugned judgment and order convicting and sentencing the Appellant, A1-Myla Rambabu and A2-Myla Muralikrishna is quashed and set aside. The Appellant, A1-Myla Rambabu and A2-Myla Muralikrishna are acquitted of the charge Under Section 8(c) read with Section 20(b)(i) of the NDPS Act.The appeal is disposed of in the aforestated terms.

CHAPTER TWENTY

AJMER SINGH VS. STATE OF HARYANA, 2010

Hon'ble Judges/Coram:

P. Sathasivam and H.L. Dattu, JJ.

Equivalent Citation: 2010(2)ACR1327(SC), 2010(88)AIC146, 2010(2)ALD(Cri)339, 2010 (69) ACC 299, 2010ALLMR(Cri)1323(SC), II(2010)CCR124(SC), 2010CriLJ1899, JT2010(2)SC185, 2010(1)N.C.C.651, 2010(2)RCR(Criminal)132, 2010(2)SCALE362, (2010)3SCC746, [2010]2SCR785, MANU/SC/0111/2010

Relevant Section/provisions: Section 20 of Narcotic Drugs and Psychotropic Substances Act, 1985

Number of Pages in the Original Judgment: 08

Case Note:

Narcotics - Contraband - Conviction - Section 20 of Narcotic Drugs & Psychotropic Substances Act, 1985 (NDPS Act) - Present appeal is filed to challenge judgment of conviction and order of sentence passed against appellant for commission of offence punishable under Section 20 of NDPS Act - Whether judgment of conviction and order of sentence under challenge deserve interference - Held, evidence on record appear to be credible and worth credence - Prosecution has succeeded to substantiate its case - There is consistent, convincing, reliable and cogent evidence on record - Court below has appraised entire evidence on record in a wholesome and harmonious manner - Impugned judgment does not suffer from any gross perversity or absurdity - There is no reason to disturb findings of conviction - Appeal dismissed.

Brief Facts:

i. The factual matrix of the case is as under: That on 24.1.1996, ASI Maya Ram accompanied by other police officials, namely, Head Constable Raja Ram and Constables Gian Chand and Shyam Singh was on patrol duty. The said police party was present near the Markanda Bridge when the accused along with another person Randhir Singh were seen coming from the side of Ismailabad. On seeing the police party, the appellant and other person Randhir Singh made an attempt to turn back and escape. However, the police over-powered them as their activities were found suspicious. Thereafter, they were served with a notice under Section 50 of the Narcotic Drugs and Psychotropic Substances Act, 1985 (hereinafter referred to as 'the Act') vide memo (Ex. PD) giving an option to them to be searched either by the Gazetted officer or the Magistrate. They signed the memo by making the choice to be searched by the Gazetted officer and they were arrested by the Head Constable Raja Ram and C-1 Gian Chand. Both of them were produced before the then D.S.P., Pehowa, Shri Paramjit Singh Ahalawat who is a Gazetted Officer, and on his direction, the bag that they were carrying was searched before him. The bag that was carried by the appellant on his shoulder was found to be containing 500 grams of charas wrapped in wax paper. Out of that, 50 grams of charas was taken as sample. Thereafter, the sample and residue were sealed separately with seal 'MR' of the Investigating Officer and 'PSA' of the D.S.P. Seal MR was handed over to HC Raja Ram while seal 'PSA' was retained by the D.S.P. himself. FIR was registered being Case F.I.R. No. 14 dated 24.1.1996 and the property was taken into possession by drawing a mahazar. The rough site plan was also prepared and the accused was arrested after informing the grounds of arrest. The statements of witnesses were recorded and challan was issued on receipt of the report of the Chemical Examiner Exhibit PH. The accused was charge-sheeted under Section 20 of the Act and he pleaded not guilty and claimed trial. The other person who was also apprehended on the same day, was also charge- sheeted and tried separately.

CASE OF PROSECUTION BEFORE THE TRIAL COURT:

i. The prosecution examined Constable Balkar Singh PW-1, MHC Som Nath PW-2, DSP Paramjit Singh Ahalawat PW-3, Head Constable Raja Ram PW-4, ASI Maya Ram PW-5 and SI Dilpanjir Singh PW-6. The prosecution also got marked the Chemical Examination Report and closed the prosecution evidence. The accused was called upon to lead evidence in defence, if any. The statement of the accused under Section 313 of the Criminal Procedure Code was recorded by putting incriminating evidence against him. Being confronted with incriminating circumstance appearing against him, the accused pleaded innocence and false implication.

ii. The case of the appellant before the Sessions Court:

a. that there was no strict compliance of the Section 50 of the Act.
b. independent witnesses not joined and associated during the search.
c. that the accused was falsely implicated in the case.

DECISION OF SESSIONS COURT:

iv. The Additional Session Judge has observed that the accused was given an option, whether he should be searched by a Gazetted officer or a Magistrate and after obtaining his option, he was produced before Deputy Superintendent of Police, who is a Gazetted Officer and on his direction the accused was searched and, therefore, there is compliance of Section 50 of the Act. Secondly, the prosecution has shown that there were enough efforts taken by the Investigation Officer to implead independent witness. Thirdly, there has been no missing link in the evidence and thus the prosecution has been able to prove the case beyond reasonable doubt that the accused "retained in his conscious possession 500 grams of charas without any permit or license on 24.1.1996". Thus, the accused was held guilty under Section 20 of the Act and was convicted vide judgment dated 5.11.1996. The accused was sentenced to undergo rigorous imprisonment for a period of ten years and a fine of Rs. 1,00,000/-(Rupees one lac). In default of payment of fine, to further undergo rigorous imprisonment for another one year.

APPEAL BEFORE THE HIGH COURT:

v. Feeling aggrieved by the decision of Additional Session Judge, Kurukshetra, the accused preferred Criminal Appeal No. 926-SB of 1997 before the High Court of Punjab and Haryana.

vi. Apart from reiterating the contentions canvassed before the learned Sessions Judge, the learned Counsel for the accused-appellant had also contended that there was delay of 15 days in sending the sample for chemical examination to FSL, Madhuban (Karnal) and no explanation is given by the prosecution for the delay caused. The High Court while considering this issue has concluded that the delay is properly explained by the prosecution.. It has further observed that, the statement of the witnesses and the report of the FSL, Madhuban shows that the sample was received in sealed cover and there was no tampering of the sample, and therefore, the said FSL, Madhuban Report must be held to have full evidentiary value.

Held, while convicting the accused:

i. The Court, therefore, concluded the principle to mean:

...it the concept simply is that, when two or more co-offenders are to be sentenced, any significant disparity in their sentences should be capable of a rational explanation.

ii. What can be inferred from the above decision is, that for applying the principle of parity both the accused must be involved in same crime and must be convicted in single trial, and consequently, a co-accused is one who is awarded punishment along with the other accused in the same proceedings. However, we are unable to apply the principle of parity to the present case as the record show that the accused Randhir Singh was convicted vide a separate trial arising out of a separately registered F.I.R. Merely because the accused Randhir Singh happened to be searched on 24.1.1996 before the same gazetted officer i.e. D.S.P., Pehowa, Shri Paramjit Singh Ahalawat, he cannot be said to be a co-accused in the present case. Further, the sentence of accused Randhir Singh was altered by the Punjab and Haryana High Court vide a separate judgment dated 3.12.2002 arising out of a separate appeal being Criminal Appeal No. 855-57 of 1999. Therefore, we do not find any merit in the contention canvassed by learned Counsel for the appellant.

iii. In view of the aforesaid findings, we do not find any infirmity in the impugned order of the High Court. Accordingly, the present appeal fails and is dismissed.

CHAPTER TWENTY-ONE

SUKHDEV SINGH VS. STATE OF HARYANA, 2012

Hon'ble Judges/Coram:

Swatanter Kumar and Madan B. Lokur, JJ.

Equivalent Citation: 2013(1)ACR1095, 2013I AD (S.C.) 29, AIR2013SC953, 2013(2)ALD(Cri)261, 2013ALLMR(Cri)764(SC), 2013(1)BLJ158, I(2013)CCR261(SC), 2013CriLJ841, 2013(2)JCC41, JT2013(1)SC212, 2013(1)MLJ(Crl)395, 2013(1)N.C.C.532, 2013(2)RCR(Criminal)232, 2012(12)SCALE699, (2013)2SCC212, MANU/SC/1124/2012

Relevant Section/provisions: Section 42 and 15 of Narcotic Drugs and Psychotropic Substances Act, 1985

Number of Pages in the Original Judgment: 09

Case Note:

Narcotic Drugs and Psychotropic Substances Act, 1985 - Section 42 and 15--Recovery of opium husk from house of appellant--Compliance with provisions of Section 42 mandatory--But no compliance--As neither secret information reduced into writing nor sent to superior--Conviction of appellant vitiated in law and unsustainable--Judgments of courts below set aside--Appellant acquitted of offence under Section 15.Section 42 of the N.D.P.S. Act, 1985 can be divided into two different parts. First is the power of entry, search seizure and arrest without warrant or authorisation as contemplated under sub-section (1) of the said section. Second is reporting of the information reduced to writing to a higher officer in consonance with sub-section (2) of that section, Sub-section (2) of Section 42 had been a matter of judicial interpretation as well as of legislative concern in the past Sub-section (2) was amended by the Parliament vide Act 9 of 2001 with effect from 2nd October. 2001. After amendment of this sub-section, the words 'forthwith' stood amended by the words 'within 72 hours'. In other words, whatever ambiguity or leverage was provided for under the unamended provision was clarified and resultantly, absolute certainty was brought in by binding the officer concerned to send the intimation to the superior officers within 72 hours from the time of receipt of information. The amendment is suggestive of the legislative intent that information must reach the superior officer not only expeditiously or forthwith but definitely within the time contemplated under the amended sub-section (2) of Section 42. This, provides a greater certainty to the time in which the action should be taken as well as renders the safeguards provided to an accused more meaningful. In the present case, the information was received by the empowered officer on 4th February, 1994 when the unamended provision was in force. The law as it existed at the time of commission of the offence would be the law which will govern the rights and obligations of the parties under the N.D.P.S. Act.In the present case, the occurrence was of 4th February, 1994. The trial of the accused concluded by judgment of conviction dated 4th July. 1998. Thus, it will be the unamended Section 42(2) of the N.D.P.S. Act that would govern the present case. The provisions of Section 42 are intended to provide protection as well as lay down a procedure which is mandatory and should be followed positively by the Investigating Officer. He is obliged to furnish the information to his superior officer forthwith. That obviously means without any delay. But there could be cases where the Investigating Officer instantaneously, for special reasons to be explained in writing, is not able to reduce the information into writing and send the said information to his superior officers but could do it later and preferably prior to recovery. Compliance of Section 42 is mandatory and there cannot be an escape from its strict compliance.As per the statement of P.W. 1, no effort was made by him to reduce the information into writing and inform his higher authorities instantaneously or even after a reasonable delay which has to be explained with reasons in writing. On the contrary, in the present case, the Investigating Officer P.W. 1 had more than sufficient time at his disposal to comply with the provisions of Section 42. Admittedly, he had received the secret information at 11.30 a.m., but he reached the house of the accused at

2 p.m. even when the distance was only 6 kilometres away and he was in a jeep. There is not an iota of evidence, either in the statement of P.W. 1 or in any other documentary form, to show what the Investigating Officer was doing for these two hours and what prevented htm from complying with the provisions of Section 42 of N.D.P.S. Act.There is patent illegality in the case of the prosecution and such illegality is incurable. This is a case of total non-compliance, thus the question of substantial compliance would not even arise for consideration of the Court in the present case. The twin purpose of the provisions of Section 42 which can broadly be stated are that: (a) it is a mandatory provision which ought to be construed and complied strictly; and (b) compliance of furnishing information to the superior officer should be forthwith or within a very short time thereafter and preferably post-recovery.

Brief facts:

i. The present appeal is directed against the judgment dated 27th March, 2008 pronounced by the High Court of Punjab and Haryana at Chandigarh in Criminal Appeal No. 802-SB of 1998. We may notice the case of the prosecution and the facts which have given rise to the filing of the present criminal appeal.

ii. On 4th February, 1994, ASI Nand Lal along with HC Hoshiar Singh, HC Suraj Bhan and other police officials were present in village Jogewala, in connection with patrolling duty. ASI Nand Lal, who was examined as PW 1, received secret information against the accused that the accused was in the habit of selling chura post (poppy husk) in his house and if a raid is conducted upon the house of the accused, the accused can be caught red-handed with the contraband. One Nacchatter Singh is stated to have been associated with the raiding party which raided the house of the accused. However, this witness was declared hostile before the Court during his examination. On conducting a search, five bags were found lying concealed under a heap of chaff in the courtyard of the house of the accused. On suspicion of having some intoxicant in his possession, the Investigating Officer served notice upon the accused Under Section 50 of the Narcotic Drugs and Psychotropic Substances Act, 1985 (for short 'NDPS Act') giving him an offer to be searched before a Gazetted Officer or a Magistrate. Accused is stated to have responded to such notice vide Ext. PC/1 where he expressed his desire to be searched before a Gazetted Officer of the police. Upon having known the desired choice of the accused, it is stated that PW1 had sent an application, Ext. PD, to the Deputy Superintendent of Police, Dabwali, through Constable Amir Singh requesting him to reach the spot. Mr. Jagdish Nagar, DSP, reached the spot after about half an hour and upon his instruction the search of the bags was conducted. From each gunny bag, 100 grams of chura post was separated as sample. The samples as well as the remaining gunny bags weighed 39 kgs. and 900 grams each and were sealed with the seal bearing impressions JN and NL, and thereafter were taken into possession vide recovery memo Ext. PE. The seal NL was handed over to HC Hoshiar Singh while seal JN was retained by the DSP himself. After completing this process, a ruqa Ex. PF was sent to the police station where the FIR being Ext. PF/1 was registered Under Sections 15/16/61/85 of NDPS Act. The Investigating Officer prepared a site plan Ext, PG. On return to the police station, the case property was handed over to the MHC with its seals intact. After receiving the test report Ext. PH from the Forensic Science Laboratory, Haryana, Madhuban (Karnal) and after completing all other formalities, the challan was filed. The challan in terms of Section 173 of the Code of Criminal Procedure, 1973 (for short " Code of Criminal Procedure ") was presented before the court of competent jurisdiction. The prosecution examined a number of witnesses including PW1 Nand Lal, PW2 Jagdish Nagar, DSP and PW Nachhattar Singh. Affidavits of Nihan Singh, Head Constable and Tejas Singh, Constable (Ext. PA and PB respectively) were taken into evidence. The accused took the plea that he had been falsely implicated in the case at the instance of Harnand Singh, Ex-Member of the Block Samiti of the area and examined four witnesses in support of his case. The Trial Court vide its judgment of conviction dated 4th July, 1998 held the accused guilty of an offence punishable Under Section 15 of NDPS Act and after hearing the party on the quantum of sentence vide its order dated 6th July, 1998 awarded 10 years' rigorous imprisonment to the accused with fine Rs. 1 lakh and in the event of default to undergo simple imprisonment for another two years. The legality and correctness of the judgment and order of sentence was challenged by the accused before the High Court.

iii. The High Court vide its detailed judgment dated 27th March, 2008 declined to interfere with the judgment of the Trial Court and while upholding the same, maintained the order of sentence, giving rise to the filing of the present appeal.

Held while allowing the appeal:

i. Thus, the present appeal merits grant of relief to the accused. We accordingly set aside the judgment of the High Court as well as the Trial Court and acquit the accused of an offence Under Section 15 of NDPS Act. We direct the accused to be set at liberty forthwith, if not required in any other case.

ii. Before we part with this file, we consider it the duty of the Court to direct the Director General of Police concerned of all the States to issue appropriate instructions directing the investigating officers to duly comply with the provisions of Section 42 of NDPS Act at the appropriate stage to avoid such acquittals. Compliance to the provisions of Section 42 being mandatory, it is the incumbent duty of every investigating officer to comply with the same in true substance and spirit in consonance with the law stated by this Court in the case of Karnail Singh (supra).

iii. The Registry shall send a copy of this judgment to all the Director Generals of Police of the States for immediate compliance. The appeal is accordingly allowed.

Videos & Tv Shows On Law & Exim

List of some important videos & TV shows on Law & EXIM by Adv. Jayprakash Somani on his YouTube Channel 'Jayprakash Somani EXIM & Legal'

Legal Videos: Hindi -English

1) SLP in Supreme Court / Special Leave Petitions in the Supreme Court of India

2) Transfer of Civil & Criminal Cases by the Supreme Court of India / Transfer of Matrimonial Cases

3) Appellate Jurisdiction of the Supreme Court of India

4) Jurisdictions of the Supreme Court of India

5) Public Interest Litigation in the Supreme Court of India / PIL in Supreme Court

6) Article 32 Writ Petitions in the Supreme Court of India

7) Bail Matters Top 10 Supreme Court Cases

8) FIR Quashing in High Court & Supreme Court

9) Bail & Anticipatory Bail Matters in Supreme Court

10) Insolvency & Bankruptcy Matters in the Supreme Court

11) Insolvency & Bankruptcy Code 2016 Part 1

12) Insolvency & Bankruptcy Code 2016 Part 2

13) Insolvency & Bankruptcy Code 2016 Part 3

14) Corporate Liquidation Process

15) Supreme Court Rules & Procedures Webinar of 2.5 hour on Zoom

16) RDDBFI Act, 1993 (Introduction)

17) The Indian Contact Act 1872

18) Negotiable Instruments Act (Introduction)

19) How to avoid matrimonial disputes& some more videos

20) SEBI Matters in the Supreme Court

21) Matrimonial Matters: Supreme Court's 20 Case Laws

22) Consumer Matters Supreme Court's 20 Case Laws

23) Service Matters Supreme Court's 20 Case Laws

24) How to Search Lawyer for Your Matter

25) Property Matters Supreme Court's 20 Case Laws

26) Bail Matters: Supreme Court's 20 Case Laws

27) Supreme Court / High Court Vacation Benches

28) 69000 Teacher's Recruitment Matters of UP Government in the Supreme Court

29) Contempt of Court Matters in the Supreme Court

30) Advocate Act's Matters in the Supreme Court

31) Business Law Matters in the Supreme Court

32) Banking Matters in the Supreme Court

33) Labour Law Matters in the Supreme Court

34) Arbitration Matters in the Supreme Court

35) Careers in Law -Zoom Webinar by Adv. Jayprakash Somani

36) Civil Matters in the Supreme Court

37) Consumer Protection Act | Consumer Matters in the Supreme Court

38) Corporate Matters in the Supreme Court

39) Criminal Matters in the Supreme Court

40) Role of Respondent in the Supreme Court of India

41) Motor Vehicle Accident Matters in Supreme Court with case laws

42) Article 131 Original Suits in Supreme Court

43) PIL in Supreme Court/ Public Interest Litigations in the Supreme Court of India'

44) CAB Citizenship Amendment Bill is not Unconstitutional

45) Supreme Court of India Cases & Process – Marathi

46) Legal Services Export / Export of Legal Services

47) Transfer of Matrimonial Cases by the Supreme Court of India

48) Public Interest Litigation PIL

49) The Specific Relief Act (Introduction)

50) Corporate Insolvency Resolution Process CIRP

51) ABMM's Career 5 - Careers in Law

52) Transfer of cases by Supreme Court

53) Writ Petitions in High Court & Supreme Court of India

54) Supreme Court Jurisdictions - Appeals, SLP, Writ Petitions, Transfer, Original, Review, Curative

55) LEGAL INDIA TV Show: Cases Handled in Supreme Court

56) Corporate Liquidation Process

57) Legal Services Export / Export of Legal Services

58) Corporate Laws

59) Election Matters- Supreme Court's 20 Case Laws

60) Companies Act, 2013

62) Competition Act, 2002

63) Banking Matters - Supreme Court's 20 Case Laws

64) Election Matters in the Supreme Court

65) Armed Forces Tribunal Matters in the Supreme Court

66) Compassionate Appointment Service matter

67) Foreign Exchange Management Act FEMA

68) Foreign Trade Policy 2021-26 Proposed

69) Customs Act 1962

70) Narcotic Drugs and Psychotropic Substances Act, 1985 NDPS Act

71) Foreign Trade Development & Regulation Act, 1992

72) How to Search Good Advocate in the Supreme Court of India

73) Sr. Adv Vikas Singh's Interview in Nani Palkhivala Wednesday Law Club

EXIM Videos: Hindi -English

1) Yes, I can do Import Export Business Easily! 36 points excellent video in Hindi

2) Yes, I can do Import Export Business Easily! 36 points excellent video in English

3) Import Export Business – Hindi video

4) Import Export Business - English video

5) Export Import Marathi TV Interview

6) Scope for Commerce Students in International Business- TV Show

7) Scope for Management Student in International Business- TV Show

8) Scope for Engineering Students in International Business – TV Show

9) Women in International Business- TV Show

10) How to do Import Export Business Successfully!'

11) Where one can get full information on Import Export Business?

12) What to do import & export?

13) Import Export Workshop/ Training/Course/ Diploma

14) How to Start Import Export Business & How to grow it. Live Webinar

15) Success Stories & Failure Stories in Import & Export Business

16) For MSME Scope in Export & Import...

17) Exports In Agri. & Food Products – English & some more videos

18) Exports to Dubai, Aabudhabii. e. UAE

19) Jewellery Exports from India

20) How to attend EXIM workshop to become excellent Exporter

21) Import Export Best Training Course – Online & Offline

22) Agri Product Export

23) Scope for Woman in International Business

24) Management Graduates Scope in International Business

25) Pharma Product's Export

26) Best Import Export Course | Practical Training | Aaronica Global Exim

27) Import Export Business for Commerce Graduates

28) How Do I Get Export Orders? Finding International Buyers

29) What Is APEDA In Import Export Business?

30) Which Is The Best Product To Export From India?

31) EXIM Remark by Manoj Kumar Faridabad

32) EXIM Remarks by Mahesh Telangana

33) What Licenses I Need To Start Import/ Export?

34) How Can I Increase My Import Export Business?

35) Which Is Best B2B Website For Import/Export Business?

36) Export Import Management with Global Marketing

37) How to Start Export Import Business | 51 Points Video

38) Scope for Commerce & Other Graduates in International Business

39) BE A SUCCESSFUL EXPORTER FOR OUR NATION - Marathi video

40) Export of Textile , Cotton, Agri., Food, & other products & services

41) Exports from MP, CG, MH, GJ & CA in Fresh Fruits & Vegetables

42) Exports in Agri. & Food Products- Hindi

43) Start your Online/E-Commerce Business

44) How to Start Export Import Business & Grow it

45) Exports in Textile & Other Products

46) Start and grow EXIM business - Live English Webinar

47)'Import Export Business!' Why, Who, What & How can one do it easily!!

48) Live: Export of Product & Services During & After Lock Down Period

49) Frauds in Import Export Business

50) Import Export for Business Man

51) Import & Export for Women

51) Import & Export for Graduate & Post - Graduate Students

52) Agriculture Exports from India

53) Digital Marketing Setup - Marathi

54) 2nd Secret of Successful Businessman

55) Digital Marketing Set up

56) Legal Services Export / Export of Legal Services

57) Export & Import with UAE

58) Service Exports / Exports by Service Providers

59) Import Export Workshop/ Training/Course/ Diploma

60) Exports & Imports with USA

61) Selection on Product for Export

62) Top Products Exported from India

63) What to do import & export?

64) ABMM Career 2 - 'Careers in Business & Industries

65) How to do Import Export Business Successfully!'

66) 5 Secrets of Successful Businessman

67) Export from MP, Chhattisgarh & Vidarbha Nagpur

68) EXIM Hindi - Textile & Apparel Export

69) EXIM Hindi - Export Import Practical Training In Delhi, Kolkata, Mumbai and Pune

70) Import Export Business

71) Import Export Business Hindi

72) Import Export Business English video

73) Import Export Business Marathi

74) Women in International Business by Exim Guru Adv. Jayprakash Somani

75) Opportunities in Foreign Trade- Adv. Jayprakash Somani's special interview

76) Textile Exports

77) India's Number in Exports. How to improve it?

78) 11 Benefits of Exim Workshop

79) Export Import Management with Global Marketing- 13 days Training Workshop

80) Cosmetic's Export

82) Export After COVID

83) Spices Exports

84) Handicraft Export

85) 10 Products India Exports to the World

List Of Adv. Jayprakash Somani's Books

1. Supreme Court of India's Leading Case Laws on 'Insolvency & Bankruptcy Code 2016'
2. Bail Matters – Supreme Court's Latest Leading Case Laws
3. Arbitration Matters- Supreme Court's Latest Leading Case Laws
4. Property Matters - Supreme Court's Latest Leading Case Laws
5. Matrimonial Matters- Supreme Court's Latest Leading Case Laws
6. Election Matters- Supreme Court's Latest Leading Case Laws
7.SEBI Matters- Supreme Court's Latest Leading Case Laws
8. Banking Matters- Supreme Court's Latest Leading Case Laws
9. Service Matters- Supreme Court's Latest Leading Case Laws
10. Contempt of Court Matters- Supreme Court's Latest Leading Case Laws
11. Consumer Protection Matters- Supreme Court's Latest Leading Case Laws
12. Corporate Law- Supreme Court's Latest Leading Case Laws
13. Supreme Court's AOR Exam- Leading Cases
14. Armed Force Tribunal - Supreme Court's Latest Leading Case Laws
15. Acquittal From 376 - Supreme Court's Latest Leading Case Laws
16. Negotiable instrument – Supreme Court's Latest Leading Case Laws
17. Contract Act- Supreme Court's Latest Leading Case Laws
18. Insider trading- Supreme Court's Latest Leading Case Laws
19. Foreign Exchange and Management Act- Supreme Court's Latest Leading Case Laws
20. Income Tax Act- Supreme Court's Latest Leading Case Laws
21. Company Law- Supreme Court's Latest Leading Case Laws
22. Competition & Monopoly Matters- Supreme Court's Latest Leading Case Laws
23. Compassionate Appointment- Service Matters- Supreme Court's Latest Leading Case Laws
24. Compulsory Retirement- Service Matters- Supreme Court's Latest Leading Case Laws
25. Voluntary Retirement- Service Matters- Supreme Court's Latest Leading Case Laws

26. Removal/Dismissal/Termination from Service- Supreme Court's Latest Leading Case Laws

27. Seniority- Service Matter- Supreme Court's Latest Leading Case Laws

28. Promotion- Service Matter- Supreme Court's Latest Leading Case Laws

29. Equal Pay for Equal Work- Service Matter- Supreme Court's Latest Leading Case Laws

30. Condition of Service- Service Matter- Supreme Court's Latest Leading Case Laws

31. Customs Act- Supreme Court's Leading Case Laws

32. Information Technology Act- Supreme Court's Leading Case Laws

33. SEC. 125 CR. P. C.- Supreme Court's Leading Case Laws

34. SEC. 498A OF I. P. C.- Supreme Court's Leading Case Laws

35. MOTOR VEHICLE ACT- Supreme Court's Leading Case Laws

36. CONDITION OF SERVICE- SERVICE MATTER- Supreme Court's Leading Case Laws

37. SUSPENSION- SERVICE MATTER- Supreme Court's Leading Case Laws

38. Reservation in SC, ST, OBC- Service Matter- Supreme Court's Leading Case Laws

39. NARCOTIC DRUGS AND PSYCHOTROPIC SUBSTANCES (NDPS) ACT - Supreme Court of India's Latest Leading Case Laws

Books are available online in India

1. Notion Press: https://notionpress.com/author/jayprakash_somani

2. Amazon: https://www.amazon.in/s?k=jayprakash+somani

3. Flipkart: https://www.flipkart.com/search?q=Jayprakash%20Somani

Books are available online at International Market

4. Amazon International: https://www.amazon.com/s?k=jayprakash+somani

5. Amazon United Kingdom: https://www.amazon.co.uk/s?k=jayprakash+somani

6. E-Books/Kindle edition at National & International Level: https://www.amazon.in/s?k=jaypraksh+somani

www.ingramcontent.com/pod-product-compliance
Ingram Content Group UK Ltd.
Pitfield, Milton Keynes, MK11 3LW, UK
UKHW021924190726
13853UKWH00002B/830

9 798887 333199